Cases in Management and

Organizational Behavior

Teri C. Tompkins
University of Redlands

Prentice
Hall

Prentice Hall, Upper Saddle River, New Jersey 07458

Senior Editor: David Shafer
Managing Editor (Editorial): Jennifer Glennon
Editorial Assistant: Kim Marsden
Assistant Editor: Michele Foresta
Executive Marketing Manager: Michael Campbell
Associate Managing Editor (Production): Judy Leale
Production Coordinator: Keri Jean
Manufacturing Supervisor: Arnold Vila
Manufacturing Buyer: Diane Peirano
Senior Prepress/Manufacturing Manager: Vincent Scelta
Cover Design: Michael J. Fruhbeis
Composition: Joseph F. Tomasso

10 9 8 7 6 5 4 3 2 1
ISBN 0-13-746389-8

To my inspiring daughters Katherine Lora-Li, age 4 1/2, and Erin Patricia Liann, age 3.

I'll love you forever
      I'll like you for always
           As long as I'm living
              My babies you'll be.
      (modified from *Love You Forever* by Robert Munsch, Firefly Books, Willowdale, Ontario, Canada, 1986.)

I know you're out there somewhere
A need so deep it reaches cross the sea
Two halves of a whole will make connection
Needing you, needing me

It was only when we gave up
Waiting for your birth(s)
We saw it had already happened
Halfway round the earth.
      (*From Needing You, Needing Me* by Anne Lawrence and Paul Roose, country songwriters and a casewriter)

Our souls have always been connected. I am overjoyed that you have given me the opportunity to sponsor part of your journey. You have already been a blessing beyond measure.

           All my love,

           Momma

TABLE OF CONTENTS

Preface

I've put this book together to fill a void that I think exists in the field of case teaching. There are not enough intermediate-length cases, especially in organizational behavior and management. Most cases available for the classroom are long, messy cases requiring total commitment to "the case method." There is rarely enough time to review and discuss theory or to include classroom exercises. The alternatives are the short cases at the end of the chapter in the textbook. These cases are usually fictional or gleaned from an article, such as found in the *Wall Street Journal*, not from direct contact with the organization and the people. They require very little thinking from students, with the "problem" and "right answer" clearly drawn from the chapter in question. These end-of-chapter cases provide little challenge for students.

The intermediate length cases in this book are messy enough that students have to think to analyze them, yet short enough that the instructor can include other teaching methods such as lecture or classroom exercises. The cases are real— the facts of the case have not been altered to make it more illustrative or plausible. Consequently, many of the cases have strong emotional undertones, which draw the students into the case and help them relate to the key characters. Students care about what happens to the people and the organization. Classroom discussion is lively. Students gain mastery of the course content because they have used course-pertinent theories and concepts, along with their own reasoning and relevant experience, to approach genuine organizational problems.

Where Can You Use This Book?

Courses in management or organizational behavior

I've included a detailed matrix referencing each case to 18 different subject chapters. There are numerous cases that would be ideal for human resources management classes, as well. The teaching notes outline questions and teaching plans that are appropriate for undergraduate, graduate, and executive levels.

As a reference book for entire business programs

The range of material in the casebook makes it an ideal reference book for many courses in a bachelor's or M.B.A. program. Cases could be used in courses of management theory, principles of management, organizational behavior, human resources management, communication, negotiation, international management, power and politics, managing change, managing diversity, ethics and social responsibility, entrepreneurship and small business, and managing conflict.

Training programs

The prepared real-life cases and teaching notes meet learning objectives that improve organizational performance. *Organizational development professionals and consultants will find a ready-made source of training materials available in the* Casebook and Instructor's Manual of Case Teaching Notes. Since the cases are intermediate length, the training group can read the case during the session without prior preparation.

Support resources

Fully developed teaching notes including detailed answers, analysis, and an explicit teaching plan for long and short teaching sessions are included in the Instructor's Manual of Case Teaching Notes. Inexperienced case teachers will find it ideal to help them learn how to teach the case. Busy professors, or ones who like to offer spontaneous activities in the classroom, will find the planning in the teaching notes very useful. This high level of support for instructors is unusual for case teaching notes.

Acknowledgments

I owe a special thanks to my dissertation chair, Professor Vijay Sathe, who sent me to gather data in organizations all over the United States and Europe, and asked me to write my first case. When I began teaching organizational behavior as a doctoral student, I was fortunate to select Cohen, Fink, Gadon, and Willets *Effective Behavior in Organizations* as the textbook. These authors taught me about a different style of case teaching. I owe my commitment to fully developed teaching plans to these authors.

I am grateful to Steve Robbins for his mentoring and support over these last three years. He helped my dream of "becoming a writer when I retire," grow into a reality at an earlier age! David Shafer, my editor, has been helpful throughout this entire project. I've also appreciated the support of Jennifer Glennon, Michelle Foresta, Judy Leale, and Kim Marsden at Prentice Hall. My good friends and research colleagues, Katherine R. Rogers, Ann Feyerherm, and Terri Egan, as well as my colleagues at the University of Redlands, have been supportive and encouraging during this intense project. I am grateful to my colleagues at Western Casewriters Association, especially my friend, Anne Lawrence, for her mentoring, and to Asbjorn Osland for his flexibility and support in reviewing and editing 17 student cases for the Western Casewriters 1999 annual workshop.

This work would not have been possible without the excellent work of my two research assistants, Amber Borden and Jonnetta Thomas-Chambers. Their tireless efforts and excellent output kept my spirits up, and improved the quality of this book and teaching note's manual. My mother-in-law, Mittie Lawrence Dick, was especially helpful during the last hours with copy editing. As a member of a generation who was thoroughly schooled in proper grammar, she gave me a lesson on the use of commas that I won't soon forget!

The cases in this book are sensitive, often painful, revealing looks at "moments in time" for the key person in the case. I am grateful to the writers and the subjects in these cases who were willing to share their stories so that students like you could learn from their experience.

Finally, I'd like to thank my family. I have learned to trust God, communicate often, be present in the moment, love openly, and laugh freely because of them. Thank you for your enduring love.

Teri C. Tompkins
Claremont, California

About the Author

Teri C. Tompkins, the eldest in a large family, was born and raised in southern California, where she has enjoyed the rich diversity of people and geography. She received her bachelor of arts and master of science degrees from California State University, Long Beach, in not-for-profit management from the Recreation and Leisure Studies department. Her mother often asked her if she was still majoring in "fun." She held several positions in youth agencies including the Girl Scouts of the U.S.A.

In 1983, she quit her job to train and qualify for the 1984 Olympic archery trials. The experience gave her confidence to change careers. She enrolled in the M.B.A. program at the Claremont Graduate University (CGU). As a research assistant for Professor Vijay Sathe, she began researching and writing cases. She subsequently enrolled in the Ph.D. program, and used cases as part of her dissertation research. Upon graduation from CGU, she joined the faculty at the University of Redlands, and became involved in the Western Casewriters Association, where she became president from 1995 to 1996.

She is the founding editor of an electronic journal on organizational learning, published by the Institute for Organizational Learning and Creating (IOLC) in Texas. She consults in the areas of team development and learning. Her interests include writing biographies for children, and anything to do with nature including, hiking, biking, and natural science. After delaying parenthood for years, she and her spouse are thoroughly enjoying raising two daughters, ages three and four.

Case Analysis Guideline

There are generally two kinds of cases in this casebook, decision cases and analysis (descriptive) cases. Some cases are both. Decision cases usually require that you identify the problem(s), evaluate solutions, and *decide* what you would do supported by rationale. Analysis cases do not really pose any problems and, therefore, require that you *explain* the behavior in the case.

Your instructor may use cases in class and not expect any preparation from you. At other times, your instructor may request prior preparation before coming to class, such as reading the case, and answering questions. If more extensive preparation is requested or a written assignment is given, these guidelines may be useful.

In decision cases, you may follow a certain "formula" to get the most out of the case. The steps in the formula are a general guideline and may be altered by your instructor based on course objectives. In analysis cases, you seek to explain "why" certain behaviors happened, using appropriate theory, and supplemented with your common sense (developed from life/work experience).

The following steps should guide you in analyzing a case.

Decision Case

1. List the facts.

Sometimes it helps to list the facts chronologically, or in relationship with key characters, or in some systematic way, to check for areas that are unclear, such as case facts that are ambiguous or differences of opinion if you are working in a group. By listing the facts, you get a sense of the whole of the case. You usually do not turn this part in; it's used to get you oriented.

2. Make inferences about the facts.

From the facts, what kinds of assumptions do you make? For example, if someone worked eighteen hours a day, seven days a week for five weeks in a row, we could infer several very different reasons why that person worked so many hours. Some might say the person is a "kiss-up," or "disorganized," or "overworked," or "dedicated." It's important to state your inferences so that other people may evaluate whether they agree with you, based on their own interpretation of the facts.

Inferences are tentative probability statements that may be a basis for deciding on a course of action later on.

3. What is the problem (and why)?

After identifying the problem(s), try to analyze why they exist. This may lead to an even more critical (or basic) problem. The obvious problem or the problem stated by the character in the case might not be the actual problem that needs solving. It may be a symptom. For example, the direct problem of an employee quitting, when analyzed, might be due to poor communication with her boss, thus suggesting that poor employee relations is a more basic problem. Often there are multiple causes for a problem.

Is there additional information that you need to analyze the case adequately? A thorough analysis recognizes what information would be gathered, even if you can't actually do it for your analysis.

4. Brainstorm possible solutions to the problem.

Don't settle for just one or two solutions. Take some time to brainstorm a large quantity of solutions. Following the rules of brainstorming, don't evaluate them until you've generated a sizable amount.

5. For each alternative, list positive and negative consequences.

    By evaluating the costs, as well as the benefits, you can possibly modify a potential solution to overcome some of the negative consequences. It is helpful to look for more than one or two consequences. Ask yourself, what might happen to if we implemented this solution.

6. Make a decision and provide rationale for it.

    Making a decision is an important part of the analysis and often forgotten by students in an effort to analyze the problem. Tell what your decision is, the possible consequences, and why you selected the decision. Finally, describe any assumptions you made.

7. What are your "lessons learned" from the case?

    What did you learn by analyzing this case? What theoretical concepts were supported or refuted, and why? Are there any new concepts that are suggested by your analysis?

Analysis case

1. List the facts.

2. Make inferences about the facts.

3. Explain the behavior or situation in the case.

    Using theory and your own learning, explain *why* events are going on. *Link* the facts from the case with appropriate explanations using such linking phrases as "because of," or "due to," "as a result of," "an example of," "illustrates," or "the following table matches the behavior in the case with the theory." This is the most critical part of a case analysis.

4. Describe your "lessons learned" from the case.

Critical Incident Case Assignment

Purpose of the Assignment

The purpose of this assignment is to link theory and practice. Whether you have lots of work experience or little work experience, it is very likely that you have had experience in organizations. Whether it's sport teams, youth groups, churches or synagogues, friends, schools, or workplaces, you may vividly remember some of the interactions that you have had, probably because there was some emotion tied to them. This assignment challenges you to take a real-life experience that happened to you and link that practical experience to organizational behavior or management theory. Once you have written a narrative case of your experience, you will analyze your behavior, and the behavior of the other key players, based on relevant theory. Then you will develop an action plan that reconnects the theory back to practice. Thus, practice is connected to theory, and theory back to practice.

The assignment has four components. Each component requires a different cache of skills. From this exercise you will develop or improve many of your skills, including creativity, writing, critical thinking, analysis, and editing.

Directions to Complete Assignment

Step 1—Notes to get you started.

*Do step 1 in bullet point; it is not necessary to write complete sentences.
Length: No assigned length, but be thorough. You must do all the substeps ("a" through "f" as follows).

(a) Pick a "dilemma or decision" that happened to you at work in which you were puzzled, confused, angry, shocked, hurt, extremely happy, proud, or any strong emotion. If you have limited work experience, choose another setting. Without judging your writing style or grammar, describe the dilemma or decision as completely as you can. Write out as much of the detail as you can remember about the "dilemma" or "decision." Include as many of the senses as you can remember. Use bullet points.
- Sounds
- Sights
- Smells
- Emotions
- Conversations
- Even tastes and textures, if applicable

(b) Think of the other <u>key</u> players. Step back and put yourself in their place. Try to describe the critical incident from their perspective. Write how they might have experienced it, using vivid description. Describe the key players (including yourself) in terms of demographics and psychosocial issues: age, race, education, gender, work experience with the company, leadership style, personality, beliefs, and so on. You may find that you do not need to include all the key players, or you may need to describe more key players.

(c) Using bullet points, outline the history that led to the event and the history after the event. In Step 2, case narrative, you can edit your history to eliminate all but the most important points. The important points should help the class understand the "critical incident" from your perspective and the key players.

(d) Describe the context in which this event happened. That is, for what kind of group or organization did the key players work? How large is the company or group? What kind of business is the company in or what is the purpose of the group?

(e) Decide if you need to include any exhibits to help clarify the case, such as simplified organizational charts, a diagram of the office, or a copy of a letter or memo (you can disguise confidential information or names).

(f) Write an epilogue telling us what actually happened after the critical incident.

Evaluation criteria for Step 1—Notes to get you started

- You did the assignment thoroughly including information in points a, b, c, d, e, and f.
- Your critical incident is focused and can be vividly described. It isn't about a whole year in your life. It is about a key event that may have been preceded by a year in your life (background, history, and contextual information).

Step 2—Narrative

Your assignment is to write an interesting case using the notes from Step 1. The case is in narrative story form; that is, you weave the facts together in a story.
Length: 7 to 12 double-spaced pages.

Look over your notes from Step 1. How can you weave this case together to make it interesting to your classmates? **Write the case in PAST tense. Use third person** (she/he <u>NOT</u> I/we). Describe yourself and others from an objective viewpoint. In other words, don't just tell us that the other person is stupid, mean, and nasty, but **SHOW** us by the person's words and actions. Be truthful; don't make up people or events.

You may disguise the case by changing people's names or other identifying information that you don't want others to know about. You may choose to describe the company in generic terms (e.g. the company produces high-end electronic equipment). You can make up a name, such as Internet Computer Company, or you can use real names of people and the company.

You will be graded on proper grammar and editing. Use 12 point type (preferably Times New Roman, Helvetica or Ariel). Indent every paragraph five spaces or one tab. Double space between line but not between paragraphs. Include plenty of subheadings (at least four). Everything should be written in past tense, <u>including</u> descriptions of the people and the company, even if this feels awkward. Everything must be written in third person, including descriptions of yourself. If you disguise names, use regular names (not names like Mr. Troublemaker). Avoid names that can be confused with another character (e.g., Al and Albert—change one of their names for clarity to another name, e.g., Chuck).

The easiest way to write a decision-focused case is to:

1. Start out with one paragraph describing you, the decision maker, wondering what to do. For example, "Paula Jones, human resource manager for XYZ Company, sat at her desk wondering what to do. Two of her best warehouse employees had nearly started throwing blows."
2. Write a background section describing the context of the critical incident. This includes information about the company, the group or location, the type of work the

key players do, the organizational culture, norms, or quirks, and the product or service. This is usually about three to seven paragraphs.

3. Write a section describing the key players. Depict the psychosocial background of the decision maker and the other key players. Usually this requires one to three paragraphs per player for the two (or three) major key players and a few sentences for any other key player. Only a few words are usually needed for minor players.

4. Describe the critical incident in detail.

5. End with a final paragraph portraying the decision maker as still wondering what to do. Do so **without telling us what the decision maker decided.**

6. Write a part B that tells what the decision maker (you) did.

7. Write an epilogue about what happened to the key players and, if relevant, to the company or group. The epilogue catches us up to the time you wrote the case. If you don't know, catch us up to the time when you lost contact.

Other Ways to Organize Your Case

If you had cooperation from the other key player(s), you could interview the other person(s) and put the case in your own, and the other person's words.

Not all cases are decision focused. Some cases (as you will find in this casebook) are descriptive narratives that illustrate theory in an interesting way.

Format of Step 2—Narrative

1. You may use this format for decision-focused or descriptive narrative cases.
2. Title of case narrative (think of a descriptive title).
3. By "your name."
4. Include page numbers at bottom center.
5. Double space.
6. Write an interesting opening that catches the reader's attention.
7. The main body of the story should include enough detail to allow your instructor or a peer review group to understand the problem you faced. It should be interesting to read with dialogue or description that might cause the reader to feel your emotion when the event happened to you.
8. Conclude your case narrative by leaving the reader "hanging," wondering what to do. (You can write what you actually decided or did in a short "B" case).
9. In an **epilogue**, write what is happening to the company and the main players at this moment in time, or the last you heard about them.
10. **Research Methodology:** Describe whether the narrative was based on your own recollections, or any written documents, or interviews with fellow workers, or any other method you used to collect your material.
11. **Industry**: A brief one- or two-sentence, description of the industry in which the narrative took place. For example, "small manufacturing plant (160 employees) of high-end electronic equipment; union employees; company disguised/not disguised."

Grading criteria for Step 2—Narrative

- The case describes a critical incident as explained in Step 1.
- The organization of the case is clear and easy to follow.
- It is written in past tense.
- It is written in third person.

- It is not pejorative. You don't tell the reader that the person is stupid, evil, manipulative, and so on. Instead, you illustrate his or her behavior and words, and let the reader draw his or her own conclusions.
- There is enough detail in the case for someone who has no experience with your organization (e.g., the professor) to develop some hypotheses or a list of factors that might explain the behavior. That is, you include enough background information about the company and the key players to help the reader see the context in which the critical incident unfolds, but you don't overwhelm the reader with minutiae.
- It is interesting to read.
- The case should be approximately 7 to 12 double spaced pages, not including the exhibits.
- You included an epilogue.
- You followed the suggested format.

Step 3—Analysis

Your assignment is to analyze the case narrative based on principles of management and organizational behavior theory from your textbook and related readings. Emerging from the issues in your case narrative, choose three topics from the list "Potential topics for case analysis" (or if a relevant topic is not on this list, talk with your instructor). For each chosen topic, write three questions, using the format suggested in the list entitled "Types of Case Questions." Use three different types of questions (e.g., cause-and-effect, challenge, and hypothetical questions) within each topic. Label each question (e.g., "hypothetical"). After each question, answer the question thoroughly. Remember to cite appropriate references (author, year, page number), when information is used from your textbook, other books, and articles.

For example, imagine you have to make a decision about how to handle two warehouse employees who nearly fought on the job. First, you would outline the factors that (you think) caused the behavior. Then suppose you found out that one of the employees had a problem with anger, which may be drug related. You could talk about violence in the workplace (from your textbook or reference material). Next, you discover another factor, that is, the two men were from different cultural backgrounds. You could use Hofstede's cultural differences to explain those factors. Then, you would outline possible alternatives of how you might handle the situation. Discuss the positive and negative aspects of each alternative. Finally, you would want to suggest the best course of action to follow based on what you have learned from the organizational behavior theories and your work experience.

Length: 7 to 12 double-spaced pages, and long enough to explain the behavior in the case. This would be difficult to do in less than seven pages, as the case analysis should include at least three topics, with three questions within each topic.

After receiving feedback from your instructor and/or peer review group, using your textbook, and other course materials from management theory, human resources, or organizational behavior courses, make notes about the theory that seems to be most connected to your experience. Focus on *explaining* behavior or suggesting *answers* to a dilemma. Write your analysis by asking yourself *why* the key players responded as they did. Use the theory to explain why or to suggest an action plan.

Format of Step 3—Analysis

1) Analysis of "title of case," followed by your name.
2) Double space, 12 point font (preferably Times-Roman, Helvetica or Ariel).

3) Include page numbers at bottom center.
4) **Key topics** (the three topics you focused on, and any additional topics you covered).
5) **Abstract:** A 250- to 500-word abstract of your narrative to help the professor remember the case when examining the analysis. An abstract is a summary that briefly tells the reader about the whole case, including case B, if applicable.
6) **Questions and Answers** Topic 1: List the topic (e.g., Motivation or Conflict).
   a) Question 1 (label the type of question, e.g., evaluation or hypothetical—see "types of case questions" attachment).
      i) Answer Question 1.
   b) Question 2 (label type of question, should not be the same type of question as Question 1 or 3 for Topic 1).
      i) Answer Question 2.
   c) Question 3.
      i) Answer Question 3.
7) **Questions and Answers** Topic 2 (same format as Step 6).
8) **Questions and Answers** Topic 3 (same format as Step 6).
9) **References:** Please provide a thorough, APA-style citation for each reference used to support the answers to your questions.
10) **What I learned:** Include a paragraph about what you learned from the analysis of the case narrative.

Grading criteria for Step 3—Analysis

- You select and analyze the most critical factors that influenced the behavior described in your case.
- Your questions follow the format suggested in the "types of case questions" attachment.
- The questions that you asked can be answered by reading your answers to the questions.
- You use relevant theory to explain case factors or to suggest why an action occurred or a decision was made.
- You use at least three different theories, which are not closely related, to explain the behavior described in the case. For example, three motivation theories would count only as one theory.
- You demonstrate your understanding of each theory by how you apply it to your analysis. You use the terms correctly and illustrate the theory appropriately, linking it to case facts.
- Your analysis is clearly written and focused.
- You include a plan of action or a reflection of how you might have done things differently if you knew then what you know now.
- Your action plan considers the pros and cons of various options. Your reflection also considers other paths you might have taken and why you didn't.
- You followed the suggested format.

Step 4—Final version of case

Edit and revise the case narrative and case analysis from Steps 2 and 3 based on student (peer review group) and professor input. Turn in the original copies of Steps 1, 2, and 3 that were edited by the professor and two clean, edited versions based on your revisions. On the clean, edited versions please mark the changes you made from the "graded" narrative and the "graded" analysis.

Grading criteria for Step 4 - Final Version of Case

- Based on everything you have learned in class to date, rewrite or edit the products of steps 2 and 3.
- Most narratives of case facts need additional information to support the final analysis and action plan, for there is often missing data in the written case that need to be added. You would need to take out editorial comments that look like analysis and move them to the analysis section.
- If your analysis included some case facts, then they should have been moved to the case narrative section.
- You included all sections requested by your professor, including the original graded papers from Steps 1, 2, and 3.
- You used three different types of questions for any one topic.
- The narrative and the analysis will be judged on the same criteria as before, except with higher expectations that you know more than you did when you wrote the first draft. Just because you got A's on the other steps does not guarantee you the same grade on your final version. Your instructor assigned grades, on the first part, based on what you knew then. It is assumed that, by the end of the course, you will have learned more and refined your thinking, which should be reflected in the final version. Some students have highlighted, with yellow pen, the areas they particularly want the professor to see in their refinements. Please pick some method to show the changes you have made between your graded narrative and analysis compared to the final version.
- Turn in **two** copies of your final version (including exhibits), one marked up (highlighted) version and one clean copy.

Types of Case Questions

When writing questions, please use a variety of cognitive questions that move from simple questions to those that require more thought. Bloom (1956)[1] developed the following system of ordering questions from lower to higher thinking skills.

These types of questions are especially good for <u>descriptive cases</u> or for the <u>theory part of the decision-focused case.</u>

Knowledge skills (remember previously learned material such as definitions, principles, formulas): For example: "Define *contingency design*." "What are the five steps to decision making?"

Comprehension skills (understanding the meaning of remembered material, usually demonstrated by restating or citing examples): "Explain the process of feedback." "Give some examples of Groupthink."

Application skills (using information in a new context to solve a problem, answer a question, or perform a task): "How does the concept of Hertzberg's hygiene factors explain the workers' dissatisfaction?" "Given the workers' satisfaction, how would you explain the outcome?"

Analysis skills (breaking a concept into its parts and explaining their interrelationships, distinguishing relevant from extraneous material): "What factors affected the emergent behavior of the team?" "Point out the major arguments Skinner would use to explain this individual's behavior."

---

[1] Bloom, B. S., and others (1956). *Taxonomy of Educational Objectives.* Vol. 1: *Cognitive Domain.* NY: McKay.

Synthesis skills (putting parts together to form a new whole; solving a problem requiring creativity or originality): "How would you organize the leadership of this team in light of new research on emergent leadership?" "How would you overcome barriers to organizational learning?"

Evaluation skills (using a set of criteria to arrive at a reasoned judgment of the value of something): "To what extent does the proposed reorganization resolve the conflict?" "If bonuses were banned, what would be the implications for the political environment at this firm?"

There are other ways to explore the case by balancing the kinds of questions you ask.

The following types of questions are especially good for <u>decision-focused cases.</u>

Exploratory questions probe facts and basic knowledge: "What case facts support the theory of Maslow's hierarchy?"

Challenge questions examine assumptions, conclusions, and interpretations: "How else might we account for the behavior of Dr. Sinclair?"

Relational questions ask for comparisons of themes, ideas, or issues: "What premises of Dubinski's are not taken into account by Coleman?"

Diagnostic questions probe motives or causes: "Why did Ferguson not confront his boss about Fester?"

Action questions call for a conclusion or action: "In response to Coleman's ultimatum, what should Sculley do?"

Cause-and-effect questions ask for causal relationships between ideas, actions, or events: "If top management moved this team onto the factory floor, what would happen to its playfulness?"

Hypothetical questions pose a change in the facts or issues: "If the three men did not have similar background factors, would the outcome have been the same?"

Priority questions seek to identify the most important issue: "From all that you have read in this case, what is the most important cause of the conflict?"

Summary questions elicit syntheses: "What themes or lessons have emerged from your analysis of this case?"

Potential Topics for Case Analysis

Managerial Careers, Management Skills

Stages in careers; career anchors; management roles; people skills; entrepreneurship versus management

Decision Making, Creative Problem Solving

Perception; optimizing decision making model; alternative decision making models; determinants of attribution; satisficing; intuition; participative decision making; electronic meetings; interacting; brainstorming, nominal, Delphi techniques

Ethics, Diversity

Ethical dilemmas; rationalizations; ethics training; social responsibility; whistle-blowing; work force diversity; gender; comparable worth

Individual Differences

Biographical characteristics; ability; personality; locus of control; learning theories—behavioral, cognitive; values; attitudes

Critical Incident Case Assignment

Motivation, Rewards

Theories of motivation; maslow; Theory X and Theory Y; hygiene factors; high achievers; expectancy theory; underrewarding employees; job satisfaction; MBO; performance-based compensation

Self-Concept, Norms, Roles

Group structure; types of norms; conformity; status; role identity/perception/expectations/conflict

Group Dynamics and Work Teams

Identity, cohesiveness, trust; self-managed work teams; virtual teams; committees and task forces

Group Development and Group Interdependence

Phases, competency, group status, differentiation; intergroup relations

Communication and Conflict Management

Key communication skills; process of communication; networks; grapevine; barriers to effective communication; feedback; functional versus dysfunctional conflict; sources of conflict; conflict handling intentions; benefits and disadvantages of conflict

Power, Influence, Negotiation

Bases and sources of power; power tactics; power in groups and coalitions; empowerment; resource dependency; dependency; distributive/integrative bargaining; third-party negotiation roles

Leadership

What is leadership; trait theories; behavioral theories; Fiedler's contingency model; path-goal theory; situational leadership theory; leader-member exchange theory; charismatic leaders

Organizational Culture, Structure, and Design

Institutionalization; culture characteristics; factors that determine, maintain, and transmit culture; division of labor; unity of command; line/staff authority; span of control; departmentalization; mechanistic and organic structures; Mintzberg's five design configurations; matrix structure; organizations in motion—growth versus decline

Technology and Work Design

Information technology; job redesign; job enrichment

Organizational Learning and Change

Diffusion of knowledge and skills; innovation; stimulants to change; resistance to change; Lewin's model; work stress; stress management strategies; organizational development; OD interventions

Managerial Functions: Planning and Control

The planning process; types of plans—short and long range, strategic and operational; approaches to planning; contingency planning; forecasting; scenarios; benchmarking; budgetary control; types of control—feedforward, concurrent; feedback; internal versus external control; operations management and control

Managing Human Resources

Job analysis; interviewing in selection; performance simulation versus written tests; performance evaluation; training and development programs

<u>Productivity: Individual, Group, and System</u>

Absence rates; turnover; job fit; job analysis; role perception and satisfaction; socialization; reducing ambiguity; matching structure to mission

<u>Globalization and Stakeholders</u>

Multinational corporations; environmental influences – economic, legal, political, and educational; strategies for international business; cultural dimensions; union-management interface

Opportunity for publication

About 50 percent of the cases published in this casebook were written by students like yourself. If you have written an interesting case and analysis, please consider submitting it for the next edition of <u>Cases in Organizational Behavior and Management.</u> Please include all the information suggested in the format for the case narrative and analysis.

It is preferred that you submit an e-mail attachment of your final edited version (case narrative and analysis) along with contact information (phones, address, e-mail address, school or work affiliations). Save as a Word document for Windows. Submit to <u>tompkins@uor.edu</u>.

We will contact you within a day or two to acknowledge receipt. If you do not receive confirmation within three weeks, please resubmit your e-mail asking if your submission was received. **Or** submit an IBM-formatted, disk copy and printed version of your final edited version (including the case narrative and analysis with questions and answers). Please include all your contact information (phone, e-mail, address, school or work affiliations).

<u>Submissions sent by the U.S. Postal Service should be addressed to:</u>

Professor Teri C. Tompkins, Ph.D.
Submission to Cases in Organizational Behavior and Management, 2nd edition
University of Redlands
P.O. Box 3080
Redlands, CA 92373

<u>Submissions sent by UPS or FedEx should be addressed to:</u>

Professor Teri C. Tompkins, Ph.D.
Submission to Cases in Organizational Behavior and Management, 2nd edition
University of Redlands
1200 Colton Avenue
Redlands, CA 92373

Matrix of Cases and Subjects

P = Primary Topic

Subject columns:
1. Managerial Careers, Management Skills
2. Decision Making, Creative Problem Solving
3. Ethics, Diversity
4. Individual Differences
5. Motivation, Rewards
6. Self-Concept, Norms, Roles
7. Group Dynamics and Work Teams
8. Group Development and Interdependence
9. Communication and Conflict Management
10. Power, Influence, Negotiation
11. Leadership
12. Organizational Culture, Structure, and Design
13. Technology and Work Design
14. Organizational Learning and Change
15. Managerial Functions: Planning and Control
16. Managing Human Resources
17. Productivity: Individual, Group, System
18. Globalization and Stakeholders

Case Title	Pg	1	2	3	4	5	6	7	8	9	10	11	12	13	14	15	16	17	18
A New Magazine In Nigeria		X			X	P				P	P			X	X	X			P
A Team Divided Or A Team United?			X		X		X	P		X	P					X	X		
Costume Bank		P										P	X		X	P			
Donor Services Department in Guatemala		X				P							P	P	X	X		P	P
Fired!		P				X											X		
Handling Differences at Japan Auto				P		X		P		P		P							
Heart Attack																	P		
Jenna's Kitchens, Inc.			P													P			
Julie's Call: Empowerment at Taco Bell								X					P	P	X				
La Cabaret				P			P			X				P					
Moon Over E.R.													X				P		
No, Sir, Sergeant!							X												
Pearl Jam's Dispute With Ticketmaster										P	P	P				P			
Problems At Wukmier Home Electronic's Warehouse			P	X				X			P		P		X		P		X
Questions Matter!						P												P	
Shaking The Bird Cage			P					X	X	X	P	X	P		X	P			
Split Operations at Sky and Arrow Airlines						X			P				P		P				
Temporary Employees: Car Show Turned Ugly				X				X	X	X	P	P							
The Day They Announced the Buyout			P		P	X				P					P		P		
Unmovable Team		X			X	X		P	P			P			X	X		X	
Your Uncle Wants You!		P		X	X	P											P	X	

CASES

A New Magazine in Nigeria (A)

by Fola Doherty

Bolt from the Blue

Ifeoma Johnson, deputy editor of *Excellence* magazine, had gone to the office as usual the morning of July 19, 1989, wondering who to send out to cover a story her team had been working on. As she parked her car, one of her colleagues, Wande Richards, rushed out and shouted, "Hey, editor, do you think you could give me a raise?" "I could do with one, too," remarked Ifeoma, smiling and turning around expecting to see Charlotte, her editor. "Don't act like you don't know," Wande replied in an accusing way. "Know what?" asked Ifeoma mystified. "That you are the new editor," she said, giving her a challenging look as if daring her to deny it. "Did you fire Charlotte?" Ifeoma joked. That was when she was told about the drama that had taken place that morning. She was astounded and felt a rage building up inside her as she thought about the treatment meted out to Charlotte. She decided to go to the newsroom to confirm the story.

The Making of *Excellence* Magazine

Back in 1986, 27 year-old Charlotte had sold the idea of a weekly magazine to some wealthy journalists, turned businessmen, with whom she worked. They encouraged her to come up with a proposal and promised to provide financing for the project. She assembled a host of reporters, editors, advertisement representatives, and a handful of technical staff. Working together as a team, they produced a dummy of the magazine for the financiers who took one look at it, and in 1987, enthusiastically provided money to start the magazine. It was called *Excellence,* and it lived up to its name, at least for the first three years.

Everyone who worked for *Excellence* was fresh out of college and in their twenties. Led by Charlotte and Ifeoma, her deputy editor, they were a hard-working, committed group, determined to change what they termed the "staid face" of journalism in Nigeria. They also wanted to make this new genre of journalism in Nigeria, human-interest as opposed to news magazine, work. The offices were located in Lagos, the commercial hub of Nigeria with a population of 10 million. The magazine was distributed nationwide and it carried stories from all over the country.

Initially, the magazine was aimed primarily at women in a country where about 60 percent of its 120 million population are women. Only 25 percent of that female population was literate and even far less than one quarter of the literate female population could afford to buy a magazine or even find the time to read it. As time went on, the male readership grew larger than expected and the articles published veered toward capturing more men readers. The target audiences then became young professionals and students. This was an opportunity to boost sales by 100 percent, from 100,000 to 200,000 thousand copies weekly. Other magazines, still struggling with a circulation of between forty and sixty thousand, were no match for *Excellence*. Thought provoking and controversial feature stories, in which the writers played the devil's advocate, were published. Needless to say, angry or supportive responses from readers would come flooding in. *Excellence's* feature stories usually dominated discussions on campuses, generating heated debates for and against. The journalists at *Excellence* tried to shape social trends among youths and, judging from the feedback and circulation numbers, they succeeded. They solicited articles from their readers on various topics of interest and published those that met their standards.

Excellence magazine comprised a few sections, which targeted both older and younger readers. One such section was the 12 page interview called the *E interview*. This was an in-depth interview with individuals from all walks of life who had contributed to the development of the country or helped shape the country before and after independence from the British. Students often used the interview as a research tool for their school papers.

Excellence Culture

There was no obvious, clear-cut hierarchy in the magazine. The staff of about 20 worked from the newsroom, which was a huge open office with desks. Reporters and editors teased and bantered with one another as they worked. Music blared from the radio in the background and, once in a while, a couple would suddenly break into a dance. Charlotte might even challenge a reporter to a dancing competition. It was a relaxed atmosphere and everyone looked forward to going to work. The staff would sometimes stay in the office after hours, far into the early morning, talking and arguing about everything from politics to potty training. All of them, except for Charlotte, were in their early twenties and had graduated from colleges in Nigeria but did not know each other before working at *Excellence*. They attended a number of high profile, social events together, and a lot of the youths began to identify with them and see them as trendsetters, both professionally and socially.

Remuneration was based on qualification, experience, story ideas, and contributions to the publication. The number of bylines obtained by staff also counted when time came for the twice a year salary review. Increments were based on the number of cover stories done and contribution of story ideas. Staff were rewarded with cash awards and sponsored vacations. Every member of the staff, including the drivers in the circulation department, got to contribute opinion pieces. These pieces, entitled *My Turn* were supposed to be either funny or serious but had to be about you, the writer. It was one of the best features of the magazine. *Excellence* staff was constantly encouraged to be more outgoing because the editor felt that meeting people was the best way to hear about and investigate interesting stories for the magazine.

A board of directors to whom the editor reported headed the magazine. The chairman of the board was the publisher, the major financier. The board met twice a year to review the general activities of the magazine. It did not, at least initially, interfere with the day-to-day running of the magazine. The editor was given free rein, and the board was happy as long as the profits came in. *Excellence* became the largest selling magazine in the country in six months and held on to that position for three years until dissatisfaction set in.

Three of the four members of the board of directors of the magazine were former journalists, who worked in hard-core newsmagazine organizations. The chairman was George Mba, a rotund man in his forties who was once a popular journalist. He dabbled in business, found it more lucrative, and abandoned his journalism career. He maintained a monthly column in a newsmagazine but concentrated mainly on his growing business. All of the other members of the board, Graham Adu, Rashid Tijani, and Winston Peters appeared more interested in the financial profit and the social clout, which they felt they could garner from being the proprietors of a magazine like *Excellence*. They expressed no interest in the lifestyle of the staff or the contents of the magazine until it became very successful.

Charlotte Demuren

The editor, Charlotte, the oldest of 13 children, always used to joke about her brothers and sisters. "We could form a soccer team and represent Nigeria. That was my parents' intention when they gave birth to us," she would say. "That was supposed to be their contribution to the development of the country." Her father died when she was in high school in Mali, where she was born. After the death of her father, the family decided to move to Nigeria where they had relatives whom they felt could help them out. On getting there, they realized that they were not going to get any help from relatives who were as impoverished as they were. Through hard work and the kindness of friends, Charlotte won a scholarship to attend college in the United States, and then returned home to help her mother educate and raise her siblings. She was very hard working and ambitious. She often shared her dreams of owning a magazine and using the proceeds to help people like herself who wanted to obtain an education but did not have the wherewithal to do so.

She was very easy to work with and had the capacity to motivate her staff. She had lured some of her staff from the competition with a promise of starting something fresh and challenging, and being paid well to do so. She lived up to her promises. The other members of the staff were recent college graduates who she said did not have any "journalistic bad habits." She felt she could mold them to fit the culture of the magazine. The former acted as mentors to the new hands and showed them what it took to work in the magazine. Charlotte was genuinely interested in her staff outside of work and was often affectionately referred to as "'mother hen," even though she was only 28 years old, just a few years older than most of the staff members.

She was a good writer and a shrewd businessperson who always came up with ideas about how to attract more advertising for the magazine. She wrote a popular self-titled weekly column in which she discussed any personal thing that came to her mind. Nothing was too sacrosanct or private for the column, including very personal matters and painful memories of her childhood. A majority of the letters from readers about her column commended her writing skills and expressed how much they could identify with her. They also said they looked forward to reading the column every Monday. But a cross section of others felt it was too personal and urged her to discontinue it or tone it down at least. She did neither and this decision would later come back to haunt her.

Ifeoma Johnson

Her deputy, Ifeoma, was invited on board from a newspaper, *The Statesman*. She had graduated from college in 1983, at 19 years old, and was beginning to make her mark as a correspondent there. The job at *Excellence* had come at a perfect time when she was growing disillusioned with her job at the newspaper. She handled the features section of *Excellence* magazine, came up with story ideas, and made sure everybody had their stories ready in time for the magazine to go to bed. She acted as editor whenever Charlotte was on vacation. She was also responsible for organizing the annual recognition and awards night for members of the staff who had contributed the most to the growth of the paper.

Both of them had met earlier as students and had forged a friendship based on mutual respect. The friendship grew as they worked together and Ifeoma was Charlotte's bridesmaid at her wedding. They worked well together as a team and encouraged the staff to do so, too. Everyone who worked there felt like they belonged to one family. "It was a genuine and good feeling," Ifeoma observed to anyone who cared to listen. She would often listen to Charlotte's dream of publishing her own magazine. Then both of them started discussing the possibility of starting it together if they ever won the lottery. They never took themselves seriously because they felt it was a dream that would never materialize.

Problems from Interference

The cohesiveness among the staff of the magazine, however, was replaced by trepidation, complaints, and anger on both sides in the weeks prior to July 1989. The more successful the magazine became, the more the publisher meddled in its editorial content. If a story was not favorable to his friends or business partners, he ordered it expunged from the magazine before it was printed. He ordered that all articles and pictures be sent to his office for approval before publication. He became increasingly critical of Charlotte and her staff, accusing them of using the magazine to "publicize" themselves especially with the *My Turn* column.

The publisher said they appeared too frequently in photographs in "society columns" of other publications around the country. He accused Charlotte of having a "hidden agenda" and warned her that the board was opposed to her using the magazine as a launching pad for herself. She was accused of using her column to garner publicity and promote herself and her friends. She denied this and told them that she was doing her best for the magazine and did not see any need to change. She explained to him that she felt the key editors of the magazine should be glamorous, well known, and "seen around town" in order to fit the image and culture of the magazine while promoting it. She refused to tone down the appearances and told them it was free publicity for the magazine. "In any case," she concluded, "the magazine was doing well in the market so we must be doing something right." The situation deteriorated and both sides were soon set on a collision course.

Ifeoma's Decision

The morning of July 19, 1989 Ifeoma heard that Charlotte had come to the office prepared for work as usual but had been prevented from entering the premises of the magazine. "Orders from above," the security men explained. Handing her a cardboard box, they told her the publisher wanted to see her in his office. "What is inside here?" she inquired, wondering why she was given the box. "We do not know," replied the security men. "We were told to give it to you," they said, trying to shield themselves from her gaze. She took the box, got back in her car and wondered what was going on. She was angry but decided to go to the publisher's office anyway. Upon arriving there, the reception was unusually cold. Her heart missed a beat as she was handed a letter. She took it with trembling hands and walked out of the office without any fuss. She was in a daze - she suspected what was in the letter but hoped she was wrong. She decided to go home; it seemed like the safest place to be.

After listening to her colleague's accounts and opinions of the incident, she went to her desk and sat there for some time, wondering what to do about her new promotion. Meddling in editorial decisions of journals was becoming the trend among publishers and proprietors in the country. They often punished editors who did not give in to their frivolous demands, and Ifeoma felt this ought to stop. If she accepted the appointment, that would send the wrong signals to them. On the other hand, being the editor of a magazine was a lifelong dream and this was an opportunity to fulfill it. She had two options, accept it and continue working in an environment that was bound to be uncomfortable but challenging, or refuse it and start worrying about how to survive until she found a new job. It was a tough decision to make but she knew what she would do.

[Do not read Part B until instructed.]

A New Magazine in Nigeria (B)

Shorty after hearing about Charlotte's dismissal, Ifeoma went to her house to see how she was holding up. She found Charlotte huddled in a corner of her bedroom with the torn envelope and termination notice at her feet. She was crying like a cowed 6-year-old, "wallowing in self-pity," she later called it. As she cried, she found it hard to believe that she had been treated so shabbily. She wondered where her career was headed, which at that time seemed like nowhere.

Ifeoma had made up her mind about what to do. She was not going to accept her promotion. She handed her letter of resignation to the publisher and gave up that month's salary in lieu of notice. The board members were caught unawares; they had not expected this move at all. The publisher invited her over for a chat and asked her to reconsider her decision. The publisher offered to increase her pay and benefits, but she stood by her decision. They wanted to know her reasons for not taking up the job. She told them that she felt Charlotte had been unjustly treated and, as a matter of principle, she was not prepared to work for an organization that treated its staff in such an unjust and shabby manner. Ifeoma told them that she also did not want her name on the masthead of a magazine where the final decisions about its contents were not hers. She said she felt she was promoted to Charlotte's position in order to spite her, not because they felt she was qualified to do the work. She explained that she came to this conclusion by judging from the way Charlotte was dismissed.

Ifeoma added that the board's constant interference in the editorial content of the magazine was stifling creativity and making it difficult to write balanced stories. Working in that kind of environment, she told them, was not her idea of journalism. Finally, she told them that out of a sense of loyalty to her friend, Charlotte, and a sense of fair play, she could not comfortably assume the responsibility. The publisher pleaded with her but she refused to reconsider her decision.

Birth of a Dream

Out of a job with nothing to do, Charlotte and Ifeoma brainstormed on what their next steps should be. They were, however, encouraged by the tremendously positive response from their readers who had grown to be fans. The readers felt they had been treated badly and wrote to the publisher expressing their opinions. They felt Ifeoma's resignation was a very noble thing to do and commended her for it. They both got a lot of letters sympathizing with them and offering suggestions about finding new jobs. Some of the jobs were worth considering while the others bordered on the ridiculous. It was the readers' way of making light of the situation. Some of their readers even sent them money and foodstuff "to get them through the rough days ahead," they said. The response was overwhelming.

A group of businessmen got together and offered to provide financing for a new magazine, promising to let them have a free hand and run it the way they wanted. They said they believed in their professionalism and the capabilities of the two women and promised not to interfere with the day to day running of the magazine and its content. After arguing back and forth, and debating on the merits of the offer, the two colleagues opted to start scouting for funds for their own magazine and then invited the businessmen to invest. They agreed to the offer. The friends, now partners, raised some money from other sources, invited a few corporate investors, and launched a magazine called *Eminence*. It was a human interest magazine, very similar to *Excellence* but with a few variations. They also made sure to put themselves on the board of directors of the magazine with enough votes to sway decisions whichever way they wanted.

As soon as the editorial staff from *Excellence* heard of the new magazine, they began to resign from their jobs and apply to come on board *Eminence*. Shocked at the influx of the staff from *Excellence*, they both pleaded with them not to abandon "the baby," *Excellence* but the staff insisted they did not want to be a part of it anymore. "It is not the same without you," they said.

All the editorial staff left with the exception of one. Together, they went on to nurture *Eminence*, which soon overtook *Excellence* to become the best and most widely circulated magazine in the country. The new venture shared its profits with the needy, and established a seniors' home in conjunction with some of its corporate financiers. It granted scholarships to those in need and gave out food to the homeless during the holidays.

A Team Divided or a Team United?

by Marlene Lowe

August 15, 1994, was a beautiful, warm, humid Chicago day. Dan and Madeleine were waiting for the meeting to be called, which would explain why Mark was not in the office. They knew why Mark was not in but wanted to hear the official version. The team's secretary rounded them up for a meeting in the president's conference room. Although it was warm outside, it was freezing in the conference room. Dan and Madeleine sighed and sat around the large walnut table in soft leather chairs. They grumbled between themselves saying things like, "Let's see how she handles *this*."

Claire, the sales/marketing manager and their boss, greeted everybody cheerfully as she entered the room. Several of the support staff returned her greeting, but Dan and Madeleine ignored her. Claire initiated some small talk before she broke the news; she said, "Mark's not here today because we had to let him go. He wasn't making his revenue numbers and things weren't working out. It's best for everybody. I do have some good news. We've hired a new person, named Sharon Marello, and she will be starting on Monday."

Jenny gasped. It was apparent that she was shocked. Although Dan and Madeleine were not surprised by the news or how it was delivered, they were angry that their teammate and friend Mark had been fired, and they were incensed that Claire tried to make it appear that it was the best for all involved. What made them even more angry was that in the same breath, they were told that Sharon was starting on Monday.

Claire's Point of View

Claire was 35 years old, single, and a native of Evansville, Indiana. She had received her B.A. in business from University of Miami, Ohio, and a master of international business from Thunderbird International School of Business. She joined Marketing Research Int'l in 1992 in the marketing department, and six months later, she took the position of sales and marketing manager in Global Services (GS), the international division. She had three direct reports, Dan, Mark, and Madeleine, whom she had hired in August and September 1992. This was her first experience directly managing people.

She was pleased to see her team working well together within the first three months. In the first year, each team member had achieved his or her revenue target. However, she suspected that there was some dissatisfaction in the team, and she thought most of it was instigated by Mark. Whenever there was a complaint about policy or how the team was managed, it usually came from Mark, and the team backed him up. He continually played the devil's advocate. A group decision was always a drawn-out process because of his interruptions and barrage of questions. Claire thought that Mark created a disruptive atmosphere, and that the team was being led astray. Also she knew that behind her back Mark called her "boss lady," which infuriated her. Claire believed that Mark's insubordination was a disruption to the team.

By mid-1994, it appeared that Mark would not reach his year-end revenue targets. Upon consulting with her boss, Claire decided that this would be the opportune time to dismiss him. She had never personally fired an employee before and was somewhat uncomfortable with the thought. But Claire realized that this would be the best way to solve her problem. Although it would be a relief for her personally, she was concerned about the impact it would have on the team. Based on conversations she overheard, it was clear that her team had not only an excellent business rapport, but they also developed a social relationship outside of work. She did not want the firing of Mark to impact her team negatively. However, since she believed that Mark was poisoning the team's morale, she felt that while it would be difficult for the team initially, in the long run it was in the best interest of the team to let Mark go. She was apprehensive, and perhaps even scared, to break the news to the team because she felt the team would be angry. But she knew she had to do it.

Mark's Point of View

Mark was 30 years old, single, and a native of Chicago. He received his B.A. in economics from the University of Michigan and earned his master of international business from Thunderbird, just as Claire had. Prior to joining GS, he was a sales representative for Xerox. He also had international experience with Siemans in Frankfurt, Germany, where he worked in the marketing department for two years. Given his work experience in Germany, his fluency in German, and his sales experience, he knew he was the most qualified and experienced member of the team.

The morning of August 14, 1994, Mark was happy to be at work. The day before, he had what he felt was a successful meeting with Kellogg's in Battle Creek, Michigan, and was planning to work on the follow-up issues that day. Midmorning, Claire called Mark into her office. According to Mark, "She was emphatic and insecure, as usual, when she told me that because my sales performance was unsatisfactory, I had the option to either quit or be fired. In any case, I would no longer be with the company." Mark thought about his options and decided that he would rather quit than be fired. After lunch, he went into Claire's office and notified her of his decision. Claire assured him that he would be given a severance package, and that she would be willing to provide a good reference should he ever need one. He had until the end of the day to pack up his things. At the end of the day, a representative from human resources and a security guard met Mark in his cube. Mark was asked to surrender his corporate American Express card (which the human resources representative promptly shredded) and I.D. badge. Then the human resources representative asked to examine the contents of Mark's briefcase to ensure that proprietary information was not taken. Mark was then escorted by a security guard out of the building and to his car.

Mark was angry and embarrassed. When describing his anger, he said, "I was really pissed at Claire. She used poor performance as an excuse to get rid of me because I challenged her decisions. I questioned her authority and the logic of her decisions. She always said she wanted group decisions, but we knew she'd already made the decision, and wanted us to agree. She didn't care about what we thought – she wanted everyone to agree that her decisions were right. I wouldn't kiss up to her and be a 'yes' person like she wanted, and she couldn't take it."

Mark was also embarrassed by the way the human resources associate treated him. He thought it was insulting when the human resources associate cut up his American Express card in front of him and then rifled through the contents of his briefcase. He felt he was treated more like a criminal than someone who had quit his job.

In some ways, Mark felt it was a blessing in disguise. He had always wanted to start his own consulting company but had never gotten up the courage to take the plunge. He took this incident to be a cue that it was time to follow his dream.

Dan's Point of View

Dan was 27, married, and a native of California. He received his B.A. in business from the University of California, Berkeley, and at the time of this incident was working part-time on his master of marketing degree from the Kellogg School of Business. Prior to joining GS, Dan was with the U.S. part of Marketing Research Int'l in client service. He was well acquainted with the U.S. company and had an internal network of contacts who often provided him with sales leads. Like everyone else on the team, Dan was career driven. He made it known that he wanted Claire's job.

As the only two men in GS, Dan and Mark quickly bonded. Although Dan did not care for Claire's management style, which he described as authoritarian, he tried to overlook it and stay on her good side. He decided early on that he needed to manage Claire, and if done properly, she would let him work autonomously. He advised Mark to do the same, but

Mark would not listen. Dan said, "After work, over beers, I tried to convince Mark to try another angle with Claire, because it was clear that his current tactics were putting Claire on the defensive and causing more harm than good. But Mark wouldn't listen to my advice."

Dan was not surprised when Mark was forced out, but he was angry nonetheless. He knew eventually the tension between Claire and Mark would need to be resolved, and that neither was capable of finding a resolution that did not include someone leaving. Although he believed that Mark had dug his own grave, he also believed that Claire was a poor manager and made her differences with Mark personal. He knew forcing Mark out was in a sense retaliatory, and he thought it unprofessional.

Madeleine's Point of View

Madeleine was 25 years old, single, and a native of California. She had received her B.A. in psychology from Loma Linda University and earned her M.B.A. from the Drucker Graduate Management Center. Prior to joining GS, she had served as a sales representative for a small food manufacturer in Chicago, whose clients were in the United States and Australia.

Madeleine was shocked by the news. In her opinion, Mark was the most qualified member of the team. Of the three-person client service/sales team, Mark had the most international work experience, as well as the most sales experience.

Madeleine believed that Mark's dismissal was due to personality differences, not performance reasons. From the very beginning, Mark and Claire had an adversarial relationship. Mark did not respect Claire's authority. He told Madeleine that he believed Claire was inept at managing the team and the business. Madeleine felt that Claire lacked the skills necessary to manage people. Claire's responses to Mark were usually defensive and fed into Mark's belief that Claire was not the right person to manage the team. It was a vicious circle. Madeleine was annoyed with both Mark and Claire, because she felt that as well-educated adults, they should have been able to resolve their differences in a more civilized and less dramatic manner than firing Mark.

Madeleine felt part of the reason why Mark was having difficulty reaching his revenue target was because of the clients he was assigned. Client assignments were supposed to be determined by each person's grade level. Although Claire did little actual sales work, she took the two best clients in terms of revenue and prestige (Coca-Cola and Bristol-Myers). Although Dan and Mark were at the same grade level, Claire let Dan choose his clients before Mark. (Madeleine felt she did this because Dan was her "Golden Boy.") Dan chose the next best clients (Quaker Oats, Pepsico, etc.). This left Mark with the smaller, less developed clients, such as Kellogg's and S.C. Johnson. Also, Claire intentionally assigned the most difficult client, Gillette, to Mark because no one else wanted it. The Gillette account required an unusual amount of time and effort, thus leaving Mark little time to develop sales opportunities with the other clients on his list. Since Madeleine was on the bottom rung of the hierarchy, her clients were small companies such as NutraSweet and Hershey, which despite being small, tended to purchase services on a regular basis and did not require a high level of service.

Madeleine was angry because of Mark's dismissal. She believed that Claire should have told the truth. Mark and Claire didn't get along. Mark had to go, since Claire was the manager. Although Madeleine would have still been upset to see her friend fired, at least in her mind, it would have been honest. To hear Claire say that "it's for the best for all involved" was a blatant lie, because it was not the best for Mark, and Madeleine felt it was not the best for the team overall. Two months prior to the incident, Mark had bought a small house, and Madeleine was worried that Mark would not be able to keep it.

History

Dan, Mark, and Madeleine worked for Claire as a client service/sales team for Global Services, the international division of Marketing Research Int'l (one of the largest marketing research company in the world). GS was conceived in 1992. Its mission was to bring integrated, multicountry databases into the corporate headquarters of fast-moving consumer goods manufacturers. At the time, this was a leading edge concept that no one else in the industry was capable of doing. In a sense, GS was an entrepreneurial group within a larger company. There were positives and negatives to this arrangement. The positive side was that GS had the luxury of the financial backing of a large organization and the support from top management. The negative side was that there was tremendous pressure to achieve revenue goals. Marketing Research Int'l (especially GS) is a company that lives and dies by sales. However, missing sales targets for one year did not normally result in termination.

Dan, Mark, and Madeleine worked closely together for a year and a half before the critical incident. Early on, they found out that they had much in common in terms of education, sports, and the love of Chicago. Because of this, their relationship grew beyond the realm of work into their social lives. For example, Dan and Mark played doubles beach volleyball in a summer league, and Madeleine was their practice partner and cheerleader. One year when Dan and Madeleine couldn't go to their respective homes for Thanksgiving, Mark invited them to his apartment for Thanksgiving dinner. It was clear to each of them that these were strong friendships that were going to last.

On a work level, they were a cohesive team. Since the three were very competitive, enjoyed sales, and were a part of a new venture within the company, it was an exciting environment. They reveled in each other's successes and shared selling techniques, while always trying to outdo each other. Of the three of them this year, Mark was having the most difficult time making his revenue numbers. By mid-1994, Mark's numbers were below target, and it looked like it would be difficult to make them up by the end of the year.

The Friday before the incident, Mark met with Claire and her boss. They told him that he needed to shape up and make every effort to make his year-end numbers. He was asked to begin providing sales projections for each client, create a calendar mapping out sales meetings, and prior to each sales meeting, present a dry run of the presentation to them. Mark found this demeaning and realized that it was the first step toward being fired. Sure enough, four days later, he was fired.

Dan was in the office when Mark was let go, so he was aware of the situation before Madeleine. Madeleine found out when she went to Mark's apartment to pick him up for dinner. He opened the door and said he wasn't really up for dinner and celebrating her birthday because he had just been fired. Madeleine was shocked and angry. They called Dan, and the threesome met at a neighborhood restaurant to comfort Mark and celebrate Madeleine's birthday.

Costume Bank

by Karen Simon and Armand Gilinsky, Sonoma State University

In business you don't have to move physical mountains, but you can accomplish amazing feats by simply believing in your ability to do what is yours to do: the job you see in front of you.
Ray & Meyers, Creativity in Business

It was the fall of 1996 Karen Simon stood at the door of the costume shop looking at the densely packed costumes, the hats hanging from the ceiling, and boxes of accessories lining the walls. She hated to give it up—all the back-breaking work over the last seven years. But she would have to if the board couldn't find a way to bring in more operating capital and treat her with the respect that she felt she deserved as the founder and visionary of the Costume Bank.

Background

During the summer of 1983, Karen didn't dream that she would soon, quite by accident, be embarking on a career she had never imagined for herself.

After three years of nonstop academics at Santa Rosa Junior College, in Santa Rosa, California, Karen had decided to take a "fun" class. She signed up for a basic theater class, and at the first class meeting, the instructor requested that students who knew how to sew sign up for the costume class, which had a low enrollment. After some deliberation regarding her availability and schedule, Karen decided to go for it. That was the beginning of a life-long passion and commitment to theatrical costuming that culminated in the creation of the Costume Bank.

Karen's work with schools and community theater started when her mentor and teacher at SRJC, the late Lloyd Elliott Scott, asked her if she would work with him on a project with Santa Rosa's Actor's Theater in October 1984. As she became involved with theater groups and schools, she realized that there should be a resource for low-cost costumes in Sonoma County. Dwindling education budgets and the lessening of government support for the arts had created a crisis for local production companies and schools. The rates charged by commercial costume shops were usually daily and prohibitive for small companies that often needed costumes for weeks at a time. She interviewed the director of the nonprofit San Francisco Costume Bank, and decided that this was what Sonoma County needed as well. Creating an independent nonprofit costume organization would enable Karen to take advantage of foundation grant monies for the arts. It also made sense to be a nonprofit serving other nonprofits. The theory was that by being nonprofit, the Costume Bank could focus on its mission: providing authentic costumes to schools and theaters without having to go into retail to pay the rent. Also nonprofit status meant that the Costume Bank could accept donations and be exempt from income tax.

The Costume Bank had started as an exercise in a job club workshop at Sonoma State University in 1988. The participants were asked to create a business and all of its aspects in great detail. Karen's idea was the most interesting to the group, because it was an unusual idea for a business, so the Costume Bank became a business, on paper.

Karen was euphoric! What if this idea became a reality? All the details were in place. All that was needed was an enterprising person to put it together. And, as the months went by, Karen became convinced that she was that person. From the beginning, Karen felt that a nonprofit organization should operate under the same principles as a for-profit business in order to succeed. To this end, she took classes in business in addition to nonprofit and arts management.

By 1989, she had worked extensively as a costumer, first in the Santa Rosa Junior College costume shop, and then as costume shop assistant at Sonoma State University's Center for Performing Arts Costume Shop, where she worked occasionally as a temporary shop manager until 1995. She was also quite busy costuming in the community for school and little theater productions. Karen trained for four years, 1985 to 1988, in the prestigious Summer Repertory Theater, working her way up from stitcher to cutter to wardrobe mistress. She had also built up a small stock of costumes, which she stored first in a closet in her home, and later in a 10' × 10' rented storage space.

In addition to freelance costuming, she worked as an assistant store manager for a local commercial costume shop, Disguise the Limit. Karen worked in the retail costume shop for six years, starting in 1988, learning everything she could about running a retail costume business. She left in 1994 to devote more time to the Costume Bank.

Developing the Design

By September 1989, Karen was ready to formalize the costume organization. She had done her research and discovered that, although there were several commercial costume shops in the county, only one did consistent business with the local theaters and schools. It was a commercial shop with a relatively high overhead and fees to match. The most important consideration, Karen thought, as she started recruiting board members, was the accessibility of low-cost costumes to the people who needed them most, the nonprofit community theaters and schools with diminishing budgets.

Although Karen knew she could manage a retail costume business with all that entails, she felt the market was already saturated in the relatively small Sonoma County. She wanted an organization that would cater to the folks who just didn't have the budgets, so she decided to make the Costume Bank a nonprofit organization itself, so it could get funding from grants and donations in addition to charging fees for rentals and costume design.

Karen knew that competition for grant money was keen, but the need for this kind of behind-the-scenes or "secondary" arts organization was not being met in Sonoma County. Granting organizations tended to look most favorably on nonprofits that filled a need.

Karen found a bookkeeper, who volunteered to do the nonprofit paperwork, and four theater loving friends to be on the board. The original board of the Costume Bank consisted of Karen, Bill Sherman, her professor and codesigner at Sonoma State University, Patricia Gorak, a community activist, Dana Kellar, the CFO of a health food chain, and Jack Greenspun, a performer and drama therapist. In six years, the board had seen many changes: Gorak and Sherman died and Kellar resigned. By 1995, they had gotten three new members: Portia Benson, a Sebastopol jeweler, P. J. Jackson, a freelance costume designer and former costume director of Berkeley Repertory Theater, and Mary Smith, a craftsperson, teacher, and grade school costumer, which brought the current board to five members. The Costume Bank was actively seeking several more committed and involved board members.

Karen hired an artist to create a logo, designed letterhead and contracts, obtained a business phone number, and a very small ad in the *Yellow Pages*. Once the nonprofit status had approval, The Costume Bank started advertising in theater programs.

For the first two and a half years, Karen operated the business out of a storage space, now 10'×30', and her home. In 1992, she rented a 350 square foot office space and moved the costumes, sewing machines, and other supplies into it. The acquisition of the space legitimized the Costume Bank and donations poured in, in the form of costumes and volunteer labor. From day one, the Costume Bank was very busy, both renting costumes and doing design and consultation.

Building the Show

Generating enough income, however, was an ongoing problem. The rental fees being charged were half of the fees of the commercial shops, and the IRS had made operating below-cost a condition to obtaining the nonprofit status. In the beginning, Karen supplemented the revenues with her own money. Until 1994, Karen had a succession of "real" jobs in addition to running the Costume Bank. By 1992, she had decided that the organization simply had to sink or swim on its own, and she stopped supplementing the income. As long as the shop was only building two shows a year and the occasional novelty costume, in addition to rentals, this arrangement worked very well. But the business kept growing at a phenomenal rate. By August 1994, Karen no longer had the energy to work two or three jobs. The Costume Bank had become a full-time commitment and so Karen quit her "day jobs," as executive assistant to a motivational speaker and part-time store manager at Disguise the Limit, to devote herself to the organization.

Karen felt she needed to give the Costume Bank her undivided attention to see if it could survive. She knew she would not get paid at first, but that was OK. After all the years, she just wanted to know if it could really make it. Thankfully, she had a wonderful, supportive husband who encouraged her to "follow her bliss" while he supported their household with the help of, eventually, her student loans and grants.

In July 1993, the Costume Bank moved into a 950-square-foot building in back of Karen's home. With a sizable donation of costumes and accessories from a community college, the space was soon full to capacity. Karen started writing grants for much needed improvements to the facility, including new doors and a large storage shed, all of which were received.

During 1993 and 1994, Karen had great success with grant writing for equipment purchases and renovations to the costume shop. In addition to the facility improvements, three new doors and light fixtures, the Costume Bank received a Macintosh computer, a cutting table, and a sign.

A part-time shop manager, Maria Silver, was hired to handle rentals and supervise the volunteers in addition to codesigning shows. Karen was grateful for the help, but as it turned out, Maria was only interested in the "glory" and, unfortunately, did not share the "vision." To keep up with this salary, the only one being paid, the Costume Bank did twice as much business. By the spring of 1995, the Costume Bank was building five shows, clown costumes for the Luther Burbank Rose Parade, and had taken on the extra task of constructing theatrical drapes for two schools. Using the costumes for collateral, the board took out a $5,000, two-year bank loan to help pay for insurance, materials, and the occasional independent contractor hired on a per-show basis.

Karen was still not earning any money and was rapidly becoming exhausted. She was working an average of 60 hours a week in the costume shop, taking seven units in graduate school, and homeschooling her youngest daughter, a sophomore. Even with volunteer help and a paid manager, running the costume shop was a monumental job. Karen's average day began at 8:00 a.m., when she started her daughter on the lessons for the day. Then the Costume Bank's business was attended to for the rest of the day until 5:30 p.m., when Karen needed to leave for school. In an average day, Karen returned five to ten phone calls, paid whatever bills were due that day, set up rental appointments, helped rental customers, which usually took one to two hours each, and helped design, cut, and sew costumes. Several times a week, there might also be laundry and fabric dying to attend to. She arrived home at 10:30 p.m., kissed her husband good night, and dropped into bed, unless the shop was building a show, in which case, she spent half the night sewing. During this time, it was not unusual for Karen to work 18 hours a day, doing whatever had to be done, from sewing, to bookkeeping, to recruiting volunteers, to running errands, to preparing the agenda for the monthly board meeting.

She was busy every minute of the day, but she felt that if she stopped for one minute, it would all would fall apart. It thrilled her that "her baby" was growing and making money. It was making a name for itself in the local theater community, and that excited and challenged Karen. The creative aspects of the business kept her energized. The company was now commanding higher design fees, which meant better fabrics, and the possibility of more costume stock. Each time the staff "built" a show, they added to its inventory and, if they built correctly, with good-quality fabrics and linings, the inventory would last longer and be worth more in rental fees. She knew that great success was just around the corner. Even though she was constantly worried about how the bills would get paid, she knew that if she worked hard enough it would all be worth it in the end.

In 1995, she wrote 20 grants, only one ($200) of which was received. In June 1995, Maria quit, and Karen knew she would need to scale back operations to protect her health. She had developed Post Polio Syndrome from a bout of polio as a child. This turn of events was very discouraging, but Karen still felt positively that the Costume Bank would make it. She never let negative feelings get in her way for long. She soon bounced back and resumed her old schedule, recruiting volunteers along the way.

In the fall of 1995, the Costume Bank built two theatrical productions and a couple of novelty costumes. The Costume Bank was also contracted by HBO to build costumes and do alterations for its production of *Grand Avenue*. Karen had found that taking an occasional film or fashion catalog assignment helped bring in much needed revenue and did not compromise the nonprofit status, which allows a small percentage of income from for-profit ventures to support the organization's mission.

Karen took mid-December through February off because of her declining health, and promised to do more rentals and less designing and building. These months were notoriously slow in the costume business so Karen was able to scale back without any loss to the business. She did do the occasional rental but, for the most part, she rested, regrouped, and continued her graduate studies. The Costume Bank did not suffer in the least. Whereas the new client goal for 1995 had been 10, the actual number of new clients in 1995 was 45.

By the spring of 1996, The Costume Bank had scaled back to building one show but had increased rentals to about four shows a month. New clients in the first quarter of 1996 were 12.

The Performance

In April 1996, Karen started the Costumer's Guild of Sonoma County, a cooperative of Sonoma County costume designers. The guild was a great success among the costumers, all of whom were tired of working alone and craved the support and networking provided by other costumers. In addition, the guild was expected to devise a standard pay scale, which would raise recognition of the great contribution of local costumers by theaters and schools.

In July, the Costume Bank moved into the 2,000 square foot basement of the United Methodist Church in downtown Sebastopol. They felt that the new location in downtown Sebastopol offered much more visibility and opportunity for community involvement. The board had a commitment from some guild members to pay part of the monthly rent of $620 in exchange for a place to store costumes and work. The balance of $490.00 per month was an extra expense the board felt was necessary to implement long-range plans for costume classes for children and teenagers.

The summer of 1996 saw the Costume Bank doing four shows with a commitment to design five more in the fall and winter, in addition to a contract to build chorus costumes and other school and theater rentals. The board devised new rental rates and determined that production companies that wanted costumes built would pay an hourly rate of $10 to more fully cover the costs of the build.

Because Karen could not possibly keep up with all of the administrative and costume maintenance work, she recruited a volunteer to handle costume organization and maintenance. A press release was written to find volunteers to help with data entry and filing. The Costume Bank hired a bookkeeper who maintained the books quarterly for a small fee.

After the move and due to the need to generate more income, the board proceeded with its plans to provide educational costume programs to students. Mary Smith, the newest board member, offered a costume class to grades 4 through 8 through the Harmony School after-school enrichment program, and Karen wrote a grant for $10,000 for the Costume Apprentice Program to benefit high school students, which was, unfortunately, denied because the foundation felt that this program could not reach enough students to justify the cost in administration and materials.

The Costume Bank saw an average increase in income of 46 percent per year in its first five years of operation (Exhibits 3-8) and continued to increase its income and rentals every year, but it was still having trouble generating enough income to thrive and pay a salary to the executive director. The board also wanted to be able to pay benefits in the form of medical/dental insurance and vacation and sick time.

Another concern was a $10,000 debt from bank loans and credit cards that the board wanted to retire as soon as possible. As the board was determined to be more involved in the actual operation of the organization, in August 1996, members implemented a new fiscal policy, which included the stipulations that the board needed to approve all equipment purchases over $100, and income statements would be done monthly instead of quarterly. In addition, the board planned two fundraising events for the fall of 1996: a rummage sale and an open house.

Strike

The Costume Bank started to fall apart in January 1997, when Karen, exhausted and ill, told the board that she would be leaving the organization as soon as someone could be found to replace her. The board was extremely upset at this news and offered to help keep the Costume Bank going by volunteering time during the week. Karen promised to make the transition as easy as possible by staying until someone could be fully oriented.

In the meantime, in order to help cut costs, the board agreed to rent out one room, currently used for costume storage, to a local theater group that needed rehearsal and classroom space.

A rummage sale was held and all nonessential costumes were sold or donated to make room for the new tenants. The executive director of the theater group shared the office with Karen and paid a portion of the phone bill and costs of operating the copy machine and fax.

Two board members, P.J. and Mary, scheduled themselves to take over rentals three days a week. Karen was still in charge of designing the spring shows and Mary offered to help with the yearly clown costumes. The board requested that Karen maintain control of the finances, paying bills and making deposits.

In May 1997 the board called a meeting to which Karen was not invited. Apparently, they felt that board members could do a better job of managing the money and keeping the Costume Bank operating. They decided that they would be in charge of all monies and how they were spent. They confiscated some rental and design payments and held them until it could be decided how they would be spent. In the meantime, Karen was paying bills under the impression that the rental and design payment money was in the bank.

Karen was angry and hurt and felt betrayed. She had always prided herself on her honesty and forthrightness with the board, and felt they were being unethical and immoral in their treatment of her. With furious passion, she confronted the board. They maintained that their decisions had nothing to do with her personally. It was business. Karen felt it was time for her first confrontation between founder and board.

Exhibit 1

Costume Bank Timeline

September 1989	Karen Simon started The Costume Bank with a rented storage space 10' × 10'.
	Filed California Non-Profit Corp. Papers.
1990	Moved to 10' × 30' storage space.
November 1991	Moved into 350-square-foot shop with office and bathroom.
July 1993	Moved into 950-square-foot shop with washer, dryer, and separate office space.
April 1992	IRS granted Non-Profit Status 501(c)3.
December 1993	Received grant for computer.
1993 to 1994	Received grants for extra storage space and improvements to space.
July 1996	Moved to downtown Sebastopol in church basement, 2000+ square feet with separate office and kitchen/dye room, and two bathrooms.
May 1997	Karen resigned.
	The Costume Bank rented half of space to pay rent.
January 1998	The Costume Bank went out of business.

Exhibit 2

Karen Simon Timeline

September 1983	Karen took costume class at Santa Rosa Junior College.
Sept. 1983 to May 1985	Karen worked in Costume Shop at SRJC.
May 1984	Karen graduated from SRJC with an A.A.
Fall 1984	Karen started doing costumes for community theater.
Sept. 1985 to June, 1987	Karen worked in the costume shop at Sonoma State University.
May 1987	Karen graduated from Sonoma State University with a B.A. in psychology and theater arts.
June 1987 to May 1995	Karen worked in SSU costume shop on as needed basis
June 1988 to August 1988	Karen worked at Summer Repertory Theater at SRJC.
Sept. 1988 to Nov. 1994	Karen worked for Disguise the Limit costume shop in Santa Rosa.
October 1994 to present	Karen worked for Disguise the Limit at Halloween.
January 1995 to May 1997	Karen went to graduate school at Sonoma State University for her M.A. in nonprofit management.
May 1997	Karen resigned from The Costume Bank.

Exhibit 3
The Costume Bank Budget 1995

	Annual Bud.	Jan.	Feb.	Mar.	Apr.	May	June	July	Aug.	Sep.	Oct.	Nov.	Dec.
Beginning Bal.		$1,036	$6,338	$5,463	$3,839	$2,146	$6,032	$4,920	$8,867	$7,759	$6,607	$4,961	$3,858
Sources													
Costume Rental	5,619	100	468	468	468	468	468	100	468	468	468	468	468
Costume Design	5,565	0	557	557	557	557	557	0	557	557	557	557	557
Consultation	4,334	361	361	361	361	361	361	361	361	361	361	361	361
Grants / Donations	10,145					5,000		5,145					
Borrowed Funds	5,000	5,000											
Total	30,663	6,497	1,386	1,386	1,386	6,386	1,386	5,606	1,386	1,386	1,386	1,386	1,386
Expenditure of Funds													
Payroll	11,500	336	958	958	1,500	958	958	500	958	958	1,500	958	958
Benefits	0	0	0	0	0	0	0	0	0	0	0	0	0
Supplies	3,799	0	380	380	380	380	380	0	380	380	380	380	380
Telephone	960	80	80	80	80	80	80	80	80	80	80	80	80
Advertising	345	0	65	20	55	20	20	20	20	65	20	20	20
Repayment of Loan	2,500			250	250	250	250	250	250	250	250	250	250
Interest	291			38	36	34	32	30	28	26	24	23	21
Gen. Admin.	9,338	778	778	778	778	778	778	778	778	778	778	778	778
Total Expenses	28,732	1,194	2,261	2,504	3,079	2,500	2,498	1,658	2,494	2,538	3,032	2,489	2,487
Net Increases	1,930	5,303	-875	-1,118	-1,693	3,886	-1,112	3,948	-1,109	-1,152	-1,646	-1,103	-1,101
Ending Bal.		6,338	5,463	3,839	2,146	6,032	4,920	8,867	7,759	6,607	4,961	3,858	2,757

Exhibit 3(continued)
The Costume Bank Budget 1996

	Annual Total	Bud.	Jan.	Feb.	Mar.	Apr.	May	June	July	Aug.	Sep.	Oct.	Nov.	Dec.
Beginning Balance			$2,757	$10,246	$8,759	$7,320	$10,147	$8,712	$7,278	$12,151	$10,720	$9,245	$12,116	$10,690
Sources of Funds														
Costume Rental	7,304	7,304	609	609	609	609	609	609	609	609	609	609	609	609
Costume Design	7,235	7,235	603	603	603	603	603	603	603	603	603	603	603	603
Consultation	5,634	5,634	470	470	470	470	470	470	470	470	470	470	470	470
Grants / Donations	20,142	20,142	5,000			5,000			5,142			5,000		
Total Sources	40,315	40,315	$9,438	1,681	6,681	6,681	1,681	1,681	6,823	1,681	1,681	6,681	1,681	1,681
Expenditure of Funds														
Payroll	15,600	15,600	600	1,300	1,300	2,000	1,300	1,300	600	1,300	1,300	2,000	1,300	1,300
Benefits	0	0	0	0	0	0	0	0	0	0	0	0	0	0
Supplies	4,558	4,558	0	456	456	456	456	456	0	456	456	456	456	456
Telephone	989	989	82	82	82	82	82	82	82	82	82	82	82	82
Advertising	380	380	0	65	20	55	20	20	20	20	65	20	20	20
Repayment of Loan	2,500	2,500	250	250	250	250	250	250	250	250	250	250	250	250
Interest	84	84	19	17	15	13	11	9	0	8	6	4	2	0
Gen. Admin.	11,971	11,971	998	998	998	998	998	998	998	998	998	998	998	998
Total Expenses	36,082	36,082	1,949	3,168	3,121	3,854	3,117	3,115	1,950	3,113	3,156	3,810	3,108	3,106
Net Increase	4,233	4,233	7,489	-1,486	-1,439	2,827	-1,436	-1,434	4,873	-1,432	-1,475	2,872	-1,426	-1,424
Ending Balance			10,246	8,759	7,320	10,147	8,712	7,278	12,151	10,720	9,245	12,116	10,690	9,266

Exhibit 4

The Costume Bank
Profit & Loss Statement
January 1994 through December 1994

Income		
Donations	$6,310.82	
Costume Design	$4,368.85	
Costume Rental	$4,322.18	
Consultation	$3,333.73	
Educational Workshops		
Grants	$2,343.00	
Sales Tax Collected	($88.00)	
Total Income		$20,590.58
Cost of Costumes		
Materials	$1,164.77	
Labor	$1,645.00	
Cleaning/Laundry	$24.00	
Total cost of Costumes		$2,833.77
Gross Profit		$17,756.81
Expenses		
Advertising	$96.00	
Auto Expense	$1,512.63	
Bank Charges	$48.90	
Fees/License	$5.00	
Office Expense	$660.68	
Su-Contractors	$410.91	
Postage & Shipping	$120.95	
Printing	$123.87	
Shop Expenses	$11,206.27	
Show Expenses	$853.91	
Telephone	$894.09	
Miscellaneous		
Total Expenses		$15,933.21
Operating Profit		$1,823.60
Other Expenses		
Net Profit/ (Loss)		$1,823.60

Exhibit 5

The Costume Bank
Balance Sheet
December 31, 1995

ASSETS
  Current Assets:
    Cash in Checking $46.09
    Grants Receivable $880.00
    Deposits on Hold $150.00
    Costume Inventory $100,000.00

    Total Current Assets $101,076.09

  Fixed Assets:
    Equipment $5,745.97
    Furniture & Fixtures $13,563.63

    Total Fixed Assets $19,309.60

    TOTAL ASSETS $120,385.69

LIABILITIES
  Current Liabilities:
    Sales Tax Payable $258.98
    Loan- Karen Simon $2,403.68
    Losan—Clair Kellar $2,285.15
    Credit Card - Capital One $964.57
    Credit Card - Citibank   ($56.67)
    Credit Card - Office Max $249.40
    Credit Card - Office Depot $2,095.13
    American Express Liab. $1,221.94
    Costume Deposits $100.00
    Bank Loan $3,128.00

    Total Current Liabilities $12,650.18

    TOTAL LIABILITIES $12,650.18

CAPITAL:
  Prior Year Surplus $111,524.73
  Loaned Capital Funds (Kellar)   ($3,000.00)
  Year-to-Date Earnings   ($789.22)

    TOTAL CAPITAL $107,735.51

    TOTAL LIABILITIES & CAPITAL $120,385.69

Costume Bank

Exhibit 6
The Costume Bank
Income Statement

	12 months, ended 31-Dec-95	
Income		%
Costume Design	$10,898.49	51.7%
Costume Sales	$3,453.10	16.4%
Costume Rentals	$5,785.00	27.5%
Consultation	$200.00	0.9%
Donations	$731.00	3.5%
Total Income	$21,067.59	100.0%
Cost of Goods Sold		
Materials	$2,250.16	10.7%
Dry Cleaning	$1,084.35	5.1%
Costumes/Wigs	$3,208.94	15.2%
Total Cost of Goods Sold	$6,543.45	31.1%
Gross Profit	$14,524.14	68.9%
Expenses		
Advertising	$174.73	0.8%
Auto Exp	$1,391.68	6.6%
Bank Charges	$138.00	0.7%
Computer Expenses	$609.70	2.9%
Conferences/Workshops	$45.00	0.2%
Dues & Subscriptions	$277.28	1.3%
Entertainment	$262.81	1.2%
Insurance	$1,191.34	5.7%
Interest Expense	$387.78	1.8%
Late Fees	$31.25	0.1%
Legal & Accounting	$105.00	0.5%
Licenses	$58.00	0.3%
Loan Fees	$266.00	1.3%
Office Expenses	$2,130.23	10.1%
Postage	$372.55	1.8%
Printing	$152.23	0.7%
Sub-Contractor	$5,048.94	24.0%
Shop Expenses	$180.07	0.9%
Show Expenses	$148.72	0.7%
Show Materials	$821.31	3.9%
Corporation Taxes	$5.00	0.0%
Telephone	$1,354.39	6.4%
Travel	$161.35	0.8%
Suspense	$0.00	0.0%
Total Expenses	$15,313.36	72.7%
Operating Profit	$1,785.11	-3.7%
NET PROFIT	$1,785.11	-3.7%

Exhibit 7
The Costume Bank
Income Statement Ending June 30, 1996

	6 months, ended 30-Jun-96	
		%
Income		
Rent	$480.00	3.4%
Costume Design	$3,867.50	27.1%
Costume Sales	$1,475.20	10.3%
Costume Rentals	$8,439.88	59.2%
Total Income	$14,262.58	100.0%
Cost of Goods Sold		
Materials	$2,079.08	14.6%
Design Fees	$569.87	4.0%
Labor	$2,585.99	18.1%
Dry Cleaning	$659.60	4.6%
Costumes/Wigs	$1,276.36	8.9%
Total Cost of Goods Sold	$7,170.90	50.3%
Gross Profit	$7,091.68	49.7%
Expenses		
Design Fees	$0.00	0.0%
Advertising	$160.00	1.1%
Auto Exp.	$775.00	5.4%
Bank Charges	$210.00	1.5%
Computer expenses	$392.78	2.8%
Entertainment	$49.75	3.0%
Insurance	$480.30	3.4%
Interest Expense	$392.28	2.8%
Legal & Accounting	$100.00	0.7%
Machine Repairs	$24.95	0.2%
Office Expenses	$1,652.16	11.6%
Postage	$35.36	0.2%
Repairs & Maintenance	$159.76	1.1%
Small Tools & Furnishings	$164.50	1.2%
Corporation Taxes	$10.00	0.1%
Telephone	$699.73	4.9%
Suspense	$0.00	0.0%
Total Expenses	$5,306.57	37.2%
Operating Profit	$1,785.11	12.5%
Net Profit	$1,785.11	12.5%

Costume Bank

Exhibit 8

The Costume Bank
Income Statement

	Historical					Pro Forma Projections				
	1990	1991	1992	1993	1994	1995	1996	1997	1998	1999
Income										
Costume Rental	$200	$1,705	$840	$1,517	$4,322	$5,619	$7,304	$9,495	$11,395	$13,673
Costume Construction	4,478	3,412	1,350	2,500	4,281	5,565	7,235	9,405	11,286	13,544
Consultation		925	6,851	4,745	3,334	4,334	5,634	7,325	8,790	10,548
Grants / Donations		125	25	2,762	8,654	15,145	20,142	25,178	30,213	37,767
Total Income	4,678	6,167	9,066	11,524	20,591	30,663	40,316	51,403	61,684	75,531
Expenses										
Payroll						11,500	15,600	20,280	26,364	34,273
Benefits								7,301	9,491	12,338
Telephone	192	320	650	557	854	960	989	1,018	1,049	1,080
Advertising	220	300	50	111	96	345	380	417	459	505
Supplies	3,300	3,500	4,642	6,085	3,688	3,799	4,558	5,014	5,516	6,067
Gen. Administration	966	1,660	2,670	4,293	14,129	12,129	14,555	16,010	17,611	19,372
Total Expenses	$4,678	$5,780	$8,012	$11,046	$18,767	$28,733	$36,081	$50,041	$60,490	$73,637
Net Profit/ Loss	$0	$387	$1,054	$478	$1,824	$1,930	$4,234	$1,362	$1,194	$1,895
Percent Inc./Dec.		32%	47%	27%	79%	49%	31%	28%	20%	22%

Donor Services Department in Guatemala (A)

by Joyce S. Osland, University of Portland

Joanna Reed was walking home through fallen tree blossoms in Guatemala City. Today, however, her mind was more on her work than the natural beauty surrounding her. She unlocked the gate to her colonial home and sat down on the porch, surrounded by riotous toddlers, pets, and plants, to ponder the recommendations she would make to Sam Wilson. The key decisions she needed to make about his donor services department concerned who should run the department and how the work should be structured.

Joanna had worked for a sponsorship agency engaged in international development work with poor people for six years. She and her husband moved from country to country setting up new agencies. In each country, they had to design how the work should be done, given the local labor market and work conditions.

After a year in Guatemala, Joanna, happily pregnant with her third child, had finished setting up the donor services department for the agency and was working only part-time on a research project. A friend who ran a "competing" development agency approached her to do a consulting project for him. Sam Wilson, an American, was the national representative of a U.S.-based agency that had offices all over the world. Wilson wanted Joanna to analyze his donor services department because he'd received complaints from headquarters about its efficiency. Since he'd been told that his office needed to double in size in the coming year, he wanted to get all the bugs worked out beforehand. Joanna agreed to spend a month gathering information and compiling a report on this department.

What Is a Donor Services Department in a Sponsorship Agency, Anyway?

Sponsorship agencies, with multimillion dollar budgets, are funded by individuals and groups in developed countries who contribute to development programs in less developed countries (LDCs). Donors contribute approximately $20 per month plus optional special gifts. The agencies use this money to fund education, health, community development and income-producing projects for poor people affiliated with their agency in various communities. In the eyes of most donors, the specific benefit provided by sponsorship agencies is the personal relationship between a donor and a child and his or her family in the LDC. The donors and children write back and forth, and the agency sends photos of the child and family to the donors. Some donors never write to the family they sponsor; others write weekly and visit the family on their vacations. The efficiency of a donor services department and the quality of their translations are key ingredients to keeping donors and attracting new ones. Good departments also never lose sight of the fact that sponsorship agencies serve a dual constituency—the local people they are trying to help develop and the sponsors who make that help possible through their donations.

The work of a donor services department consists of more than translating letters, preparing annual progress reports on the families, and answering donor questions directed to the agency. It also handles the extensive, seemingly endless paperwork associated with enrolling new families and assigning them to donors, reassignments when either the donor or the family stops participating, and the special gifts of money sent (and thank-you notes for them). Having accurate enrollment figures is crucial because the money the agency receives from headquarters is based upon these figures and affects planning.

The Cast of Characters in the Department

The Department Head

Joanna tackled the challenge of analyzing the department by speaking first with the department head (see the organizational chart in Fig. 1.) José Barriga, a charismatic, dynamic man in his forties, was head of both donor services and community services. In reality, he spent virtually no time in the donor services department and was not bilingual. "My biggest pleasure is working with the community leaders and coming up with programs that will be successful. I much prefer being in the field, driving from village to village talking with people, to supervising paperwork. I'm not sure exactly what goes on in donor services, but Elena, the supervisor, is very responsible. I make it a point to walk through the department once a week and say 'hello' to everyone, and I check their daily production figures."

Like José, Sam was also more interested in working with the communities on projects than in immersing himself in the details of the more administrative departments. In part, Sam had contracted Joanna because he rightfully worried that donor services did not receive the attention it deserved from José, who was very articulate and personable but seldom had time to look at anything beyond case histories. José never involved himself in the internal affairs of the department. Even though he was not considered much of a resource to them, he was well liked and respected by the staff of donor services, and they never complained about him.

The Supervisor

This was not the case with the supervisor José had promoted from within. Elena had the title of departmental supervisor, but she exercised very little authority. A slight, single woman in her thirties, Elena had worked for the organization since its establishment 10 years earlier. She was organized, meticulous, dependable, and hardworking. But she was a quiet, nonassertive, nervous woman, who was anything but proactive. When asked what changes she would make if she were the head of the department, she sidestepped the question by responding, "It is difficult to have an opinion on this subject. I think that the boss can see the necessary changes with greater clarity."

Elena did not enjoy her role as supervisor, which was partly due to the opposition she encountered from a small clique of long-time translators. In the opinion of this subgroup, Elena had three strikes against her. One, unlike her subordinates, she was not bilingual. "How can she be the supervisor when she doesn't even know English well? One of us would make a better supervisor." Bilingual secretaries in status-conscious Guatemala see themselves as a cut above ordinary secretaries. This group looked down on Elena as being less skilled and educated than they were, even though she was an excellent employee.

Second, Elena belonged to a different religion than the organization itself and almost all the other employees. This made no difference to Sam and José but seemed important to the clique who could be heard making occasional derogatory comments about Elena's religion.

The third strike against Elena was her lack of authority. No one had ever clarified how much authority she really possessed, and she herself made no effort to assume control of the department. "My instructions are to inform Don José Barriga of infractions in my daily production memo. I'm not supposed to confront people directly when infractions occur, although it might be easier to correct things if I did." ("Don" is a Latin American honorific used before the first name to denote respect.)

This subgroup showed their disdain and lack of respect for Elena by treating her with varying degrees of rudeness and ignoring her requests. They saw her as a watchdog, an attitude furthered by José who sometimes announced, "We (senior management) are not going to be here tomorrow, so be good because Elena will be watching you." When Sam and José left the office, the clique often stopped working to socialize. They'd watch Elena smolder out of the corner of their eyes, knowing she would not reprimand them. "I liked my job better before I became supervisor," said Elena. "Ever since, some of the girls have resented me, and I'm not comfortable trying to keep them in line. Why don't they just do their work without needing me to be the policeman? The only thing that keeps me from quitting is the loyalty I feel for the agency and Don Jose."

The Workers

In addition to the clique already mentioned, there were three other female translators in the department. All the translators, but one, had the same profile: in their twenties, of working class backgrounds, and graduates of bilingual secretary schools, possessing average English skills. (As stated earlier, in Latin America, being a bilingual secretary is a fairly prestigious occupation for a woman.) The exception in this group was the best translator, Magdalena, a college-educated recent hire in her late thirties, who came from an upper-class family. She worked, not because she needed the money, but because she believed in the mission of the agency. "This job lets me live out my religious beliefs and help people who have less advantages than I do." Magdalena was more professional and mature than the other translators. Although all the employees were proud of the agency and its religious mission, the clique members spent too much time socializing and skirmishing with other employees.

The three translators who were not working at full capacity were very close friends. The leader of this group, Juana, was a spunky, bright woman with good oral English skills and a hearty sense of humor. A long-time friend of José's, Juana translated for English-speaking visitors who came to visit the program sites throughout the country. The other translators, tied to their desks, saw this as a huge perk. Juana was the ringleader in the occasional mutinies against Elena and in feuds with people from other departments. Elena was reluctant to complain about Juana to José, given their friendship. Perhaps she feared Juana would make her life even more miserable.

Juana's two buddies (*compañeras*) in the department also had many years with the agency. They'd gotten into the habit of helping each other on the infrequent occasions when they had excessive amounts of work. When they were idle, or simply wanted to relieve the boredom of their jobs, they socialized and gossiped. Juana, in particular, was noted for lethal sarcasm and pointed jokes about people she didn't like. This clique was not very welcoming to the newer members of the department. Magdalena simply smiled at them but kept her distance, and the two younger translators kept a low profile to avoid incurring their disfavor. As one of the them remarked, "It doesn't pay to get on Juana's bad side."

The Organization of the Department

Like many small offices in Latin America, the agency was located in a spacious former private home. The donor services department was housed in the 40 × 30 foot living room area. The women's desks were set up in two rows, with Elena's desk in the back corner. Since Sam and José's offices were in former back bedrooms, everyone who visited them walked through the department. Inevitably they stopped to greet and chat with the long-time employees (Elena, Juana, and her two friends). Elena's numerous visitors also spent a good deal of time working their way through the department to reach her desk, further contributing to the amount of socializing going on in the department.

Elena was the only department member who had "official" visitors since she was the liaison person who dealt with program representatives and kept track of enrollments. The translators each were assigned one work process. For example, Marisol prepared case histories on new children and their families for prospective donors, while Juana processed gifts. One of the newer translators prepared files for newly enrolled children and did all the filing for the entire department (a daunting task). Most of the jobs were primarily clerical and required little or no English. The letter translations were outsourced to external translators on a piece-work basis and supervised by Magdalena. Hers was the only job that involved extensive translation; for the most part, however, she translated simple messages (such as greeting cards) that were far below her level of language proficiency. The trickier translations, such as queries from donors in other countries, were still handled by Sam's executive secretary.

Several translators complained, "We don't have enough opportunity to use our English skills on the job. Not only are we not getting any better in English, we are probably losing fluency because most of our jobs are just clerical work. We do the same simple, boring tasks over and over, day in and day out. Why did they hire bilingual secretaries for these jobs anyway?"

Another obvious problem was the uneven distribution of work in the office. The desks of Magdalena and the new translators were literally overflowing with several months' backlog of work while Juana and her two friends had time to kill. Nobody, including Elena, made any efforts to even out the work assignments or help out those who were buried. The subject had never been broached.

The agency was growing at a rapid pace, and there were piles of paperwork sitting around waiting to be processed. Joanna spent three weeks having each department member explain her job (in mind-numbing detail), drawing up flowcharts of how each type of paperwork was handled, and poking around in their files. She found many unnecessary steps that resulted in slow turnaround times for various processes. There were daily output reports submitted to José but no statistics kept on the length of time it took to respond to requests for information or process paperwork. No data were shared with the translators, so they had no idea how the department was faring and little sense of urgency about their work. The only goal was to meet the monthly quota of case histories, which only affected Marisol. Trying to keep up with what came across their desks summed up the entire focus of the employees.

Joanna found many instances of errors and poor quality, not so much from carelessness as lack of training and supervision. Both José and Sam reviewed the case histories, but Joanna was amazed to discover that no one ever looked at any other work done by the department. The employees were very accommodating when asked to explain their jobs and very conscientious about their work (if not the hours devoted to it). However, they were seldom able to explain why things were done in a certain way, because they had received little training for their jobs and only understood their small part of the department. Morale was obviously low, and all the employees seemed frustrated with the situation in the department. Nevertheless, with the exception of Magdalena who had experience in other offices, none of them could offer Joanna any ideas about how the department could be improved.

Figure 1

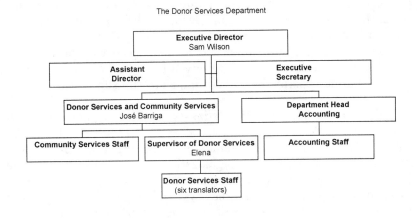

The Donor Services Department

[**Please do not read part B until told to do so by your instructor.**]

Donor Services Department in Guatemala (B)

Sam was pleased by the detail in Joanna's analysis of the department but shocked by the findings. Joanna had compiled statistics on turnaround times and productivity levels for all the local sponsorship agencies, and Sam's office was the least efficient. Joanna went back to her other projects, but a week later Sam requested that she help him implement the recommendations. He was planning to run the department for two months to familiarize himself with its workings before hiring a department head. Since an invitation to implement is the dream (or nightmare) of all consultants, Joanna accepted with the proviso that she could only spend two hours a day in the office, given her other responsibilities. In actuality, Sam had no time to run the department, and Joanna ended up supervising the department two hours a day.

Joanna started out by having staff meetings with the translators. She told them she saw no reason why they could not be a topnotch donor services department, and constantly stressed the importance of their role in retaining and attracting new donors. She told them that, as professionals who cared about the organization and its work, she expected them to work hard whether or not she or the other managers were present. She also asked them for suggestions on various changes. Although they were talkative in one-on-one conversations, they were generally very silent in these meetings. They were not used to being consulted, and they were not used to working on problems as a group. The only staff meetings they had attended in the past were inspirational talks from Sam, who was stronger on vision than nuts and bolts. Joanna wrote up revised procedures for each work process, and asked the translators for their approval before including them into a policy manual. There was no resistance to the policy changes.

Joanna redesigned the jobs of most of the translators. She split up all the community programs in the country and divided them into four geographic regions. Four translators were then named regional translators and made responsible for all the processes pertaining to their region. Juana and one of her cronies, as well as the two newest translators, were selected for these jobs. They were far more varied than the old jobs and included more opportunity to use English and have contact with community personnel. This change eliminated the overload problem and gave the translators more control over the tasks they did throughout the day. As long as they met the needs of their region, they could decide what work needed to be done when. Magdalena, as senior translator, was relieved of translating greeting cards and simple queries from other countries, a task that now belonged to the regional translators. She continued to supervise the work of the external translators and assumed the difficult donor queries formerly handled by Sam's secretary, which resulted in speedier responses. Marisol continued to produce the case histories but with help from the regional translators during crunch times. Since her work required a specialized computer, it was not possible to divide this task among the regional translators.

There was some jealousy regarding the two specialized jobs. The regional translators acknowledged that Magdalena's English was far superior to theirs. Some of them, however, coveted Marisol's job doing case histories, since they saw it as a more prestigious position. Even though her job was much more repetitive and boring than that of the regional translators, she had a special computer that symbolized status to the others. Furthermore, Sam frequently asked Marisol about her production, since it related to his growth goals. The other translators were envious of the special attention she received from the director.

To deal with their perceptions, Joanna repeatedly reassured the regional translators that their job was equally important, and they were not just a "pool" of clerical help. She focused on improving their English skills, so they would eventually be in line for the specialized jobs should they become vacant. Joanna also assigned special projects, which brought both status and growth opportunities, to the regional translators, who had their own work up to date. While there was a little resistance to the reorganization, the jobs of the regional translators were so much more interesting that they accepted the changes fairly quickly.

Elena received a new title of "community liaison" and could focus on what she did best—keeping track of communications to the communities. She was relieved to relinquish the headaches of supervision and became much more cheerful.

Joanna went over all the staff's work when she came to the office, and answered their questions. She corrected their English and explained rules of usage, so the translators not only improved their work but felt they were learning on the job. As she found fewer and fewer errors in their work, she checked it less and encouraged them to do their own quality control.

Joanna also posted two highly visible charts in order to motivate the employees and direct their efforts. One showed the priority tasks of the day, given the overall work of the department. This was done so that staff knew whether they should work on their own area or on special projects with a more pressing deadline. The other chart was a running total of the work produced, compared with the set monthly quotas, so everyone could see the variance between the two and have something to aim for. She suggested a daily quota system for the employees, but there was so much resistance to that idea that she dropped it. Going from no supervision to a quota system was too great a leap for these employees and not an appropriate suggestion for their organizational culture.

Joanna made two changes in the office layout. She moved 20 file cabinets to form an aisle leading to the back offices. This separated the translators from all but the most garrulous and determined visitors. Elena's desk was moved to the entrance to the department, so visitors did not have to formally greet everyone else on their way to her desk.

Joanna's greatest implementation error involved the newly designed workstations. Joanna and Sam collaborated to make the best use of the available space; the result was partitions with cubbyholes that were both attractive and functional. However, they prevented the workers in the two back stations from seeing other people. There was one resulting casualty; a younger translator, who reportedly had a volatile temper, quit suddenly when her work area was reassigned in the far corner of the office. Apparently, the employee interpreted this location as the bottom of the totem pole. In reality, Joanna had placed her there because she trusted her to work with less supervision than some of the others (e.g., she put Juana smack dab in front of her own desk). There was a rumor that this employee had tried to poison Joanna's beverage out of vengeance; as the story went, Juana threw the beverage away before Joanna could drink it. One of the lessons Joanna drew from this incident (other than avoiding beverages at work) was that the physical setting had a different symbolic meaning to the Guatemalans, than it did for her or Sam. She had underestimated the importance of social contact at work. She realized, in retrospect, that while the staff was content to play a rubber stamp role in the reorganization decisions, Joanna should have involved them more in the decision about workstations. She tried to remedy the problem by having the regional translators pick up and deliver work to and from other areas, so they would have some opportunities for social contact built into their day, and the discontent eventually died down.

Juana never challenged Joanna's authority, but she did have a few run-ins with other people. In each instance, Joanna took Juana aside, informed her why this type of behavior was unacceptable, and coached her on how she could have handled herself more effectively. Joanna complimented Juana on her leadership potential and pointed out that she could use this strength to be either a negative or a positive force in the office. Juana would never, however, be promoted to a supervisory position until she showed the ability to get along with other people, whether she liked them or not. In a nonjudgmental way, Joanna explained that Juana's past actions had created a climate that was unpleasant for others and worked against the organization's mission. Fortunately, Juana chose to be a positive leader and became the most outstanding of the four regional translators. Joanna praised Juana for her change of attitude and assigned her special projects, like working on a training manual, to utilize her talents. The difficulties between the clique, and the other employees disappeared almost completely.

Sam took four months to find a department head. To Joanna's surprise, he did not advertise the position; instead, members of the organization prayed for a candidate. Joanna acknowledged the wisdom of this method when they located an excellent woman with the age, experience, and language competence to inspire the respect of the translators. Joanna trained her in, cleaned out her desk drawer, and gratefully returned to her research, and her porch.

The production figures and turnaround times for the department improved significantly. The headquarters manager responsible for supervising donor services departments around the world was so amazed at the rapid improvement in the department that she came to visit the Guatemalan office. This further increased the morale of the staff—they had earned a reputation as "winners"!

Fired! (A)

by Tony Marks

Tony Marks, a sales representative for Rykoff-Sexton, Inc., was just given a written warning by his sales manager, Hank Smith, for poor performance on the job. After hearing the bad news, he sat, somewhat puzzled because he did not know his performance had been substandard. It was the first time in his professional career that he ever received such a warning from an employer. When his sales manager left the room, Tony had a chance to reflect upon what had just happened and to explore the various alternatives given to him. There was now a huge dilemma staring him in the face. Should he try to improve his performance, or realize his days at Rykoff-Sexton were numbered, and begin looking for other employment?

Rykoff-Sexton, Inc. was a nationwide corporation providing goods and services to restaurants, hotels, schools, and other organizations. Rykoff manufactured food, paper goods, cleaning supplies, and heavy equipment for use by the foregoing organizations. The company employed roughly 25,000 people nationwide. The company's regional facility was located in La Mirada, California, with its corporate headquarters located in Chicago, Illinois.

Rykoff-Sexton, Inc.

Rykoff-Sexton, Inc. was one of the largest distributors and manufacturers of goods and services nationwide. The company was founded in 1928 by Seymour Rykoff. The company was originally called S.E. Rykoff & Company, and then it later merged with Sexton Food Corporation in the late 1970s. Together they formed a partnership that has remained strong today. Rykoff's mission statement or company slogan to its customers was "Enjoy life. Eat out more often." This statement was also on their big green delivery trucks, which was one of their trademarks. Rykoff's main competitor in the marketplace was Sysco Food Service, which was the number-one distributor of goods and services in the industry nationwide.

At the La Mirada facility, where Tony was employed from October 1994 to February 1997, there were about 400 employees. The breakdown was as follows:

- 150 outside sales representatives covering the greater southern California area, including San Diego
- 50 inside sales support staff
- 150 warehouse personnel
- 25 administrative assistants
- 25 upper-level management employees consisting of:
  - 10 regional sales managers
  - 10 senior product managers
  - 5 senior executives in charge of sales for the entire branch.

Key Players

There were four main participants involved in the critical incident that took place on February 6, 1997: Rob Resnick, vice president of sales for the La Mirada facility, Hank Smith, regional sales manager for West Los Angeles, Mike Bergen, regional sales manager for the San Fernando Valley, and Tony Marks, sales representative covering both the San Fernando Valley and West Los Angeles areas. Tony worked directly under each individual for a period of time while he was employed at Rykoff-Sexton, Inc.

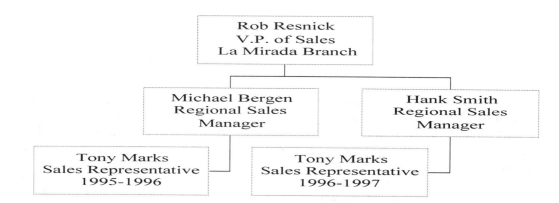

Tony, a 27-year-old Caucasian, born and raised in Los Angeles, was hired by Rykoff on October 28, 1994. Tony was a very easygoing type of guy, who always got along with everyone. His approach to being successful was to work as hard as you can, and you will be rewarded for your success. Prior to his employment at Rykoff, he was a sales and marketing representative for various distributors in the industry. He had six years of prior industry experience and sales success, which was a vital aspect of his employment. He got along with everyone he came in contact with and was always willing to help others. He was looking forward to a great career at Rykoff and thought he had made the right career decision.

Rob Resnick, a 37-year-old Caucasian, married with two children, began his career at Rykoff when he was just 22 years old and fresh out of college. He began his employment there as a sales representative and remained in that position for about eight years. At that point, he was promoted to regional sales manager for the West Los Angeles area. As a regional sales manager, he was responsible for 12 sales representatives. Each representative had a sales quota each year, and it was his responsibility to see that each of them met their respective quotas. If each of them met their yearly sales quotas, then he would receive a yearly bonus, based on how well his region performed compared to the others.

During the time Rob served as regional sales manager, he hired Tony as a sales representative to work directly for him. When Tony was hired, he underwent an intensive three-month training program that prepared him to go out onto the street to build his territory. During this time, Tony was given a salary for the first year, while he was building his territory. Although none of the sales representatives had individual territories, Tony was placed in a region that included a lot of the "heavy hitters" of the sales force. So it was hard for him to compete for the business. Tony's sales for his first year were in line with the other trainees' goals. He was in the "middle of the pack." Rob remained Tony's sales manager for the first year or so and offered his guidance and expertise on how to build a territory. He took the time to help in any way he could because he wanted Tony to have the same success that he had when he was a sales representative.

Rob and Tony also had a personal relationship outside the office. They were good friends for about eight years prior to working together at Rykoff. They met while playing on the same softball team and developed a friendship after that. Rob told Tony that if he ever wanted to come and work at Rykoff, he would get him in. So when the opportunity arose in 1994, Tony took him up on his offer and was hired to join his sales team. Prior to joining Rykoff, Tony had five years of experience in the food and beverage industry as a sales and marketing representative, so the transition was a smooth one.

After about a year of working together, Rob was transferred to another region where he served in the same capacity. Now all of a sudden, Tony was going to have a new sales manager, whom he had never met before, and he really did not know what to expect. Rob told Tony not to worry, that the new sales manager, Mike Bergen, would be a good fit for the region, and that he was a really great guy who would go out of his way to help continue the building process.

New Sales Manager

Needless to say, Tony was a bit nervous but decided to have an open mind. Mike Bergen, a 42-year-old Caucasian originally from New York, moved to Los Angeles about 10 years earlier. He was hired by Rykoff as a regional sales manager in 1992. His territory was the Ventura County area, stretching up the coast to San Luis Obispo. When Rob was transferred to another region, Mike was assigned there. Prior to joining Rykoff in 1992, Mike had worked previously for various other manufacturers and distributors in the industry, and came to Rykoff with 10 years of experience. He was the Ventura County regional sales manager until the fall of 1995, at which time he took over the West Los Angeles territory.

In the beginning, Tony and Mike worked well together. There were no major problems. He was very easygoing and his philosophy was as long as you put in a good day's work, that was okay with him. He, like Rob, was always there if Tony needed help or had a problem. After about six months of working for Mike, one of the other sales representatives in the region, Gus, quit. It was Mike's job to divide up the accounts to the other sales representatives in the region. Usually the new people get accounts when they become available because they are still trying to build up their territories and account base. However, it is at the discretion of the sales manager.

When Tony found out that certain accounts were possibly going to be available, he asked Mike which accounts he could potentially receive. Mike told him that he decided to give all of Gus's accounts to another representative who had just started with the company three months prior. He had just completed his training and had not even been out on the street yet. Tony did not think this was fair, and voiced his displeasure to Mike about it. Tony was struggling a bit to build his territory, and these accounts would have given him a much needed boost. After much persuasion and discussion, Mike agreed with Tony that he should receive some of the accounts. Thus, the accounts were divided up equally between Tony and the new representative. Relations between Mike and Tony appeared to be fine after that incident.

At the end of 1996, Rob Resnick was promoted to vice president of sales for the La Mirada facility. He was now in charge of ten regional sales representatives, and his job was to ensure that sales increased each year. When Rob was promoted, other changes were about to take place that would immediately affect Tony's future at Rykoff. With Rob being promoted, Mike Bergen was transferred to take over his region, and a new manager would be assigned Mike's territory. This would affect Tony greatly. Before Mike left the region, he and Tony had an informal meeting in November 1996. Mike told him that the company was beginning to crack down on those salespeople who were lagging behind the pack. Tony's sales were appreciably behind the rest of the salespeople in the region. However, most of the other sales representatives had been with the company at least five years. He was given an oral warning by Mike to improve his sales, or a possible disciplinary action could take place. This was only a verbal warning at that time.

In December 1996, Hank Smith took over Mike's region as regional sales manager. Hank, a 32 year old Caucasian, began his career at Rykoff in 1993 as a sales representative in the West Los Angeles region. He was promoted to regional sales manager in December 1996. Prior to joining Rykoff, Hank was a sales representative for various other manufacturers and distributors and had eight years of experience in the industry. Tony had met Hank on a number of occasions, and he seemed like a nice, easygoing guy, but they did not have a chance to work together for very long.

Difficult Factors

There were different factors that led up to the critical incident that occurred on February 6, 1997. The first factor, and probably the biggest one of all, was the fact that at Rykoff there were no set territories for the sales representatives in each of their respective regions. The sales representatives in each region were free to go wherever they could get the business. This caused them to "step on each other's toes." Sales representatives would walk into an account, not knowing if it was already being serviced by a fellow Rykoff salesperson, whether it was assigned to a person from the sales support staff, or if it was being served by the competition.

This was a huge problem for Tony as he began to build his territory from scratch. He was given a list of accounts that were, or had been, customers of Rykoff at one point in time. It also listed the last date merchandise was sold to that account, so anyone could go there to try to get the business. Tony did not mind doing this; however, his region consisted of some of the top-producing sales representatives in the company, and, of course, they got to these potential accounts first, through word of mouth from their existing customers. Tony was usually a step behind because someone had always gotten the business ahead of him. Fortunately, any sales leads that were in his region were assigned to him from the inside sales support team. So Tony built his territory from outside cold calling and leads received from the sales support staff.

Another factor that led to the critical incident was the fact that there were not enough new establishments opening where Tony could have the first chance at getting the business. He was not able to increase his business and account base, which would have generated more sales for his annual sales quota. He decided that the only way he was going to generate more sales was to increase his sales in his current accounts by selling them more goods, and by sweeping out the competition. This did work to some extent, but it was not enough to meet his quota. He tried his best, but his best just was not good enough. All of these factors occurred during a span of about a year and a half and ultimately led up to the critical day.

In January 1997, after reviewing the sales quotas for each of his sales representatives, Hank told Tony that he would like to meet with him. Upon meeting with Tony, Hank gave him a written warning for poor performance, citing that he did not meet his sales quota for 1996. He did not at any time say that Tony was in danger of losing his job, only that he needed to pick up the pace. Tony was given new monthly sales goals to achieve, and if he did not achieve them, there was a possibility that he could be terminated. Tony signed the warning letter, which went into his personnel file. We now must ask the question, "What should Tony do to meet his sales quota?" The answer was unclear.

A month after Tony received the written warning from his new regional sales manager, Hank Smith called him at home before he left on his usual route. Hank phoned to ask Tony to come into the office for a meeting. Tony had no idea what the meeting was about. Hank was very brief during the phone conversation. After arriving for the meeting, they went into the office behind closed doors. Hank informed Tony that a business decision had been made to terminate him because of continued poor performance, and for failure to meet specified monthly sales quotas. Tony pleaded his case, saying that he wasn't even given a month to make his sales quota after the written warning was issued. Hank replied by saying, "You would not have made it, anyway because your sales were too low."

Unemployed

Tony was shocked and disappointed over what had just taken place. His whole body went numb. He began to think to himself that he was, all of a sudden, unemployed. He wondered in what direction he could go. He had never been fired from a job before, so he was very disappointed and upset. He felt that he had failed in his career for the first time. At the meeting with Hank, Tony's final paycheck was waiting for him. He filled out an "exit interview sheet," which stated that he received his final paycheck and gave information on health insurance. Tony signed the paper, which brought an end to his employment at Rykoff-Sexton, Inc. Hank told Tony that he would be more than happy to give him a reference, should he need one. Hank reiterated to Tony that it was a business decision, and that it was out of his control. Tony said that there were no hard feelings.

After the meeting was over with Hank, Tony wanted to say good-bye to Rob, who originally hired him, and who was also Tony's good friend. There were no hard feelings on

Tony's part. When he got to Rob's office, his secretary told Tony that he was too busy to see him. Tony did not believe that he was too busy. He felt that Rob did not have the guts to face him because he must have been one of the people instrumental in his termination. Tony was not looking for another explanation for his dismissal. He was hoping Rob would say, "I wish you good luck in your future endeavors, and I hope there are no hard feelings. I will be happy to give you a reference." That was all Tony was looking for, but he did not get it. He was disappointed in his friend's behavior but realized that he had to move on and act quickly to find another job. He wondered in what direction he should take his career.

Fired! (B)

After taking a few days to gather his thoughts, Tony had to decide in what direction he wanted to take his career. Since he had over six years of experience working in the food and beverage industry as a sales and marketing representative, he could search for other jobs in that area, or search for a sales job in another industry. He was also considering changing fields altogether. Since he did not have a college degree, he knew that the door would be closed to him in certain industries. He remained quite undecided for about a month, when things changed dramatically for the better.

After a month of being unemployed, and after many job interviews in the sales area, Tony received a call from one of his best friends, Laird Malamed. He asked him how the job search was going, and Tony told him that he had just completed a second interview for a sales representative position with a pharmaceutical company. He told Laird that he was waiting to hear back from the company for a possible third and final interview. Laird told Tony that his father was looking for someone in the company's marketing department, and that he should call him to discuss the position. The company was in the financial industry, in which Tony had no experience.

Tony went for an interview, and after speaking with Ken Malamed, the owner of the firm and Laird's father, Tony was offered the position of marketing associate and given the opportunity to learn and be a part of a very successful and profitable business. However, there was one condition. Since Ken did not hire associates without a college degree, Tony would have to go back to school to obtain his degree. Tony agreed to this if he accepted the position. Tony told Ken that he would like to think about the offer for a few days, and Ken agreed to that. After a couple of days, Tony decided that he would accept the position. He realized that these kinds of opportunities may only come once in a lifetime, and it was a chance for a fresh start in a new and exciting field. It was also an opportunity to work for someone that Tony had known all his life. He knew that there were many new challenges ahead, but he was ready.

After Tony had accepted his new position, the pharmaceutical company called later that same day to say that he had made the third and final interview for the sales representative position. Tony never had second thoughts about accepting his new position before he heard back for a possible third interview with the pharmaceutical company. He said that he had accepted a different position but thanked the pharmaceutical company for the opportunity. In hindsight, he was glad to be getting out of sales and into a more stable working environment. He trusted his bright, new future!

Handling Differences at Japan Auto

by Nancy Zufferey

In the administrative office of Japan Auto Sales Los Angeles Parts Distribution Center (LAPDC), an incident occurred between two female associates. Acting as department specialists, these coworkers were challenged by a small, yet complex and dynamic office environment. They were also unwittingly about to change the attitudes and the way "things were run" at the LAPDC. The team's motivation was disintegrating rapidly, and after a couple of months of stifled expression and pent-up hostility, a heated and emotional argument broke out between these two associates.

Background

Japan Auto Sales is a large Japanese-owned automobile manufacturer. Japan Auto's foundations are strongly built on commitment to quality and customer satisfaction. Japan Auto holds ongoing customer service and quality classes, which every associate is required to attend. Japan Auto believes in loyalty toward its associates, and prides itself on promoting from within whenever possible. Further, Japan Auto strongly encourages continuing education. Associates who work for Japan Auto Sales and who strive for future career opportunities and growth must achieve at a minimum, a bachelor's degree. There is no possibility for an associate to excel and "move up the ladder" at Japan Auto without such a degree.

The LAPDC was the largest of eight distribution centers throughout the United States that supported Japan Auto's vast parts operations. It housed between 50 to 60 full-time Japan Auto associates and over 300 union warehouse employees. Most of the full-time associates worked in various departments of the administrative office with the exception of approximately 10 supervisors (five day shift and five night-shift) who oversaw the union warehouse associates. The administrative office was composed of one national manager, one office manager, three claims specialists, five critical parts analysts, three data entry associates, and one core and obsolescence program specialist. All specialists were at the same nonmanagerial grade level, each having his or her own area of expertise.

As part of Japan Auto's diversified work force objective, the administrative office at LAPDC had a well-balanced ethnic mix comprised of African Americans, Hispanics, Caucasians, and Asians (including one Hawaiian and one Taiwanese). Approximately 50 percent of the associates were women. Two of the female specialists, Barbara Smith and Chrys Haber, were working toward their degrees and aspired to grow within the company. Most of the male counterparts were married and all were ambitious. Further, all the men were either in college or already had a bachelor's or master's degree. Although the actual office setting was fairly casual, including casual business attire and acknowledging each other on a first-name basis, professionalism and high-quality output were a must.

For the most part, the office had an exceptional team environment. Excellent internal and external customer service was a priority. Further, career advancement was strongly encouraged and office objectives were consistently reinforced and met in the department. One of the office objectives was to have all associates cross-trained with the exception of a few associates who were waiting for retirement in the near future and did not aspire to further growth. The associates of the administrative office were pleased with this development plan. These enthusiastic associates agreed that the office operation would run more smoothly when all associates were fully cross-trained. Since the office was relatively small, this cross training would be most beneficial in events such as associate leave or disability, sickness, and vacation. Furthermore, this cross training would benefit each associate in his or her own development plan and career growth.

Barbara Smith

The argument, which took place between the two ambitious women, Barbara Smith and Chrys Haber, not only changed the attitude of both women but the office environment as well. Barbara, a woman approximately thirty years old, had been working at the LAPDC for approximately seven years. She came from an outside transportation company and started her career at the LAPDC as an office clerk. Eventually she was promoted to secretary and recently had been promoted to department specialist. She was responsible for the LAPDC's core and obsolescence programs. In her quest for career growth, she began going to college and had almost completed her general education requirements for her associate of arts degree. Although Barbara aspired to be professional and promote herself, she did not perceive herself the way fellow associates did. Her demeanor had often been misunderstood. Many times she was regarded as harsh and argumentative. She had insulted many associates by insinuating she was above them because she was attending college. She failed to remember, however, that others already had their degrees. In any event, these associates were her internal customers and they believed they should have been regarded with respect.

One day while in a meeting with the three claims specialists, Barbara warned one associate, a soft-spoken Asian lady of about 50 years old named Carolyn, that if she wanted to progress at Japan Auto or at least keep her job, it was advisable she "attend college and learn how to file." Apparently, Barbara did not approve of Carolyn's filing methods. However, Barbara did not assist Carolyn or the group by suggesting alternative filing methods. Her advice simply was to attend college to learn how to file in order to maintain employment. The other specialists viewed this statement as thoughtless, condescending, and insulting. Carolyn and the other associates involved in the meeting were taken aback by Barbara's comments and worse, Carolyn felt she had been personally insulted. Barbara's demeanor merited her the office joke that "Barbara would get her degree in filing and successfully return to her previous position as file clerk."

On another occasion, while on a dealer visit, Barbara had an argument with a dealership employee. The employee disagreed with some of the operating procedures Barbara had enforced and proceeded to offer alternative suggestions. This was quite annoying to Barbara. Instead of discussing the issue with this employee, she told him to just do as was instructed in the procedure manual.

Another complaint was that she interrupted people while they were speaking either informally or during formal conferences. She would interject her thoughts and statements, which frequently had no relevance to the discussion at hand. Behind her back she was also ridiculed because of the way she spoke. Most associates noted that her vocabulary was limited, but in trying to mimic upper management, she would use terminology she was unfamiliar with and did not understand.

Also, the other associates (some men, but mostly women) criticized her for the way she groomed herself. Many times she entered the office with clothes too tight and short for office standards, or wearing pants that were stained. The general consensus among associates was that she had a false sense of superiority and that she was professional neither in appearance nor in the working environment. With the exception of the office manager, who appeared to feel sorry for Barbara, the department tried its best to steer clear of her.

Chrys Haber

Chrys Haber was 37 years old. She had worked at Japan Auto for almost three years. However, her background was not from the LAPDC. She entered Japan Auto as an assistant for Japan Auto's Facilities Department and was given, as part of her career growth, the opportunity to work as a claims specialist for the LAPDC. She had been with the new department approximately four months. Like Barbara, in her quest for career growth, Chrys had been working toward her bachelor's degree. She quickly made friends among the associates and was well respected. Because of her background at Facilities, she was also able to assist the department with its external needs, such as ordering office equipment, getting assistance with maintenance needs and removal of hazardous materials, both in the administrative office and the warehouse. Further, she had contacts with associates in upper management who were watching her growth in the company. She was known by fellow associates and management as a high-energy, dynamic associate, and was considered an asset in the department. Moreover, her good reputation had extended to other departments within Japan Auto, and upper management felt she had potential, with proper guidance, to become an outstanding manager.

Both Barbara and Chrys were similar in that they both had very strong personalities. However, they were also quite dissimilar. First, Barbara was searching for career growth challenges in ways that were not approved of by the other associates. When new teams were being formed, such as "change" teams or "kaizen" committees (created in order to solve specific problems) Barbara would be first to volunteer as a member. The problem with this was, before understanding what the team was all about, she would criticize its purpose and come up with plans to recreate it. Associates questioned how she could improve something she knew nothing about. Her approach was viewed by most other members as a desperate attempt to prove her self-worth — always "trying to shine" at the expense of others and at the expense of office objectives. Chrys, possibly because she was a little older, was more comfortable in investigating company opportunities and had a more relaxed approach with other associates. Although eager to participate in a change or development team, Chrys chose to wait and see how her workload would accommodate such a responsibility. Second, where Barbara was not very critical of herself, Chrys was quite judgmental of herself. Chrys always analyzed the claims system and would frequently discuss alternative methods with specialists to improve such aspects as computer and communication systems. She regularly sought input from peers, dealers, and the manager regarding her performance. Moreover, she was meticulous about her person, conscientious of how she dressed and presented herself. Third, Barbara remained on her own, quietly working in solitude on projects outside of her division and frequently reminding other associates of her growth, whereas Chrys strongly believed in teamwork and ownership that encompassed associate feedback and open communication.

Although there was always something about Barbara that was untrustworthy and annoying to Chrys, she decided that, as a new associate in the department, she would have to wait and see what the reasons might be for her feelings. It didn't take long for her to find out. In the cross-training procedures, Barbara was to learn the operations of the claims department and each of the three claims specialists would learn Barbara's area of expertise, the core and obsolescence programs. The first claims specialist to transcend over to the core and obsolescence programs was Carol, who learned quickly and diligently. However, Barbara was not very willing to partake in the claims training, even though it had been written in the fourth-quarter objectives for the office. She would always have an explanation for not participating in the training. Often she would come in to work 20 to 30 minutes late and immediately start working at her own desk.

Team Training

Finally Carolyn, the claims specialist who had been chosen by the office manager to train Barbara in claims, expressed her concern by gently asking Barbara why she was not actively participating in the training. Barbara sharply responded, "I have too much work of my own to do. I'll do my training when I have time." For the second time, Carolyn felt she had been personally disrespected and insulted. Chrys, who overheard the conversation, felt that Barbara was not doing her part in the team's effort toward achieving the office objectives. Moreover, she felt that Barbara was acting very selfishly and against one of Japan Auto's primary mottoes—teamwork.

Based on what she had observed, Chrys sensed that Barbara was taking advantage of Japan Auto in that she expected the most from the company, but she was not willing to do her part.

Most employees believed that Barbara enjoyed creating training plans and office presentations. As it turned out, instead of learning claims operations, she had been working on PowerPoint presentations for her own personal gain. The office manager, Marcia, an intelligent yet insecure 38-year-old female, was sympathetic toward Barbara. She could see that Barbara was desperately trying to be different and move ahead. Marcia was constantly afraid of hurting others' feelings. Moreover, she always strove for acceptance by each and every associate, so instead of guiding and encouraging Barbara to follow the development plan, she allowed Barbara to do as she pleased. This created major hostility among several associates who were also eager to promote themselves, including Chrys. Basically, the sentiment among associates was "why should one person have the opportunity while others who also have motivation, experience, and talent do not get the same opportunities?" Whether intentional or not, Marcia's actions clearly stated that favoritism existed in the office environment. Interestingly enough, Marcia managed to create antagonism and feelings of lack of loyalty—exactly the opposite of what she wanted.

Communicate with Barbara Directly?

One morning during a coffee break, a few associates approached Chrys to complain about Barbara. One by one, they enumerated the various ways they had been "burned" by her. Chrys, who had been working in the department for approximately two months by that time, asked the associates if they had ever discussed their feelings with the manager. It turned out that the associates were afraid to speak up because they did not wish to create any office disturbance by complaining. They also sensed that the office manager favored Barbara. However, they were tired of Barbara's attitude and lack of team spirit and hoped Chrys might speak for the group. Although Chrys agreed that Barbara was taking advantage of the group, she did not feel comfortable in speaking to the manager right away, especially as a group representative. First, because she was so new in the department, she felt that she might be overstepping her boundaries as a newcomer. Second, she did not think it was appropriate to discuss such matters with the manager without first giving Barbara the benefit of discussion. Therefore, Chrys suggested that as an initial step, the complaints should be addressed directly to Barbara, and if the situation could not be resolved, the conflict could be taken one step further. The associates thought this would be a good idea and asked Chrys, since group consensus was she had good communication skills, if she would represent the group and speak with Barbara in private.

Chrys was quite apprehensive about the "task" she had accepted. She felt she was on unfamiliar turf and, unsure of how Barbara might respond to the upcoming confrontation, she tried to formulate and rehearse what she wanted to discuss at the meeting. Late that afternoon, she approached Barbara and asked her for a moment in a conference room. The two went behind closed doors and Chrys proceeded to explain the sentiments of the group. She then explained the department's position, and her own, that it was only fair that Barbara do her part in the cross training. Barbara became hostile and started yelling at Chrys, telling her that she had no right discussing department complaints with her. She reminded Chrys that she was in college and did not need assistance from a new associate on how to interact with others. Chrys's retort was that she was in college as well, and that college experience and education had nothing to do with professional office demeanor nor departmental goals. Chrys warned Barbara that her "patronizing tactics were not threatening" to her. The argument became rather heated as Chrys descriptively enumerated the many ways in which Barbara had antagonized fellow associates as well as herself.

Instead of strictly adhering to the original goal of resolving the office conflict, Chrys took the situation defensively and personally. She had allowed herself to be provoked by Barbara's earlier comments. As such, her priority evolved into a determination not to let Barbara "win" the argument. Although Chrys remained calm externally, she was inwardly shaken and furious. She stood up from her seat and bent forward to look over Barbara and told her it was her duty in the department to do her share, which was to learn claims—a demand from office management. Chrys further threatened that if Barbara had a problem maintaining her share in the plan, the issue could be taken to management. Chrys, still leaning over Barbara, accused her of antagonizing and insulting the department, and informed her that her demeanor in general was not recognized as appropriate. She ended her insults to Barbara by sternly suggesting that if Barbara wished to progress in her career, the first and vital step would be to take real college classes and "learn how to communicate with others—a necessary element in all facets of career development."

The attack injured Barbara's feelings. Teary eyed, she backed down and apologized to Chrys. However, that was not enough. Chrys demanded that she apologize to each and every associate in the department. Barbara promised to hold a meeting with the associates the next day. The following morning, all associates, as one group, entered the large conference room to meet with Barbara. At that one-hour meeting, each associate had the opportunity to "vent" and discuss how to work as a team without future hostilities. Two of the associates were still unnerved by the conference for a few days after the meeting. However, it took great courage for Barbara to go through with the meeting, which fortunately ended in accord. With a few exceptions, most associates agreed that the bottom line was that the department must work as a team—unified—in order to reach its objectives.

Chrys Evaluates the Confrontation

Although Chrys's anger and confrontation had a positive impact on Barbara's attitude and behavior, she did not feel good about the situation as a whole. She remained deeply disturbed by her actions and questioned why and how one individual could make her so angry. She had never behaved so cruelly and aggressively toward a fellow human being. Was it a question of ethics—one employee abusing sentiments of team members and an office manager for one's personal gain? Or was the anger based on personal, emotional, and competitive reasons? Not only did Chrys feel she had digressed to the same level as Barbara, but, in practicing her skills at leadership, she felt that she had let herself and the group down by not acting "professionally." Her anger had escalated during the initial meeting and she realized that she had let her pride and personal emotions get the best of her—she had lost control. And although Chrys had gained the reputation of being a loyal and fair associate as well as strong team leader, what remained in her conscience was an underlying sense of guilt and embarrassment at how the meeting had evolved and been reconciled.

After the incident, Barbara tried to befriend Chrys. As a matter of fact, to her surprise, Barbara confessed that she had been intimidated by and looked up to her. Barbara voluntarily learned her share in claims, and whenever there was a question regarding company policy or office improvements or procedures, she respectfully approached Chrys or the other associates.

Although Barbara was never completely accepted by the other associates, she made marked improvements in her work style and manner. Although many associates were still wary of her, it was clear to all that she was trying to get along as a team player. She maintained better office conduct and restrained herself in times of possible conflict with other associates. Many associates, including Chrys, wondered if the office manager had found out about the incident. It seemed that since the confrontation, when there was a question regarding office procedures or when training sessions were being scheduled, Marcia would first ask Chrys if she would like to attend. Further, Marcia took away many of Barbara's presentation privileges. At the group's last staff meeting, Marcia announced that she would be initiating "a different course of action for the department" that would not entail presentations. Was it possible that Marcia realized that the group sensed favoritism, which would detrimentally affect the team's spirit and objectives?

Chrys learned quite a lot from the experience regarding her new environment, office behavior, and feelings. Upon reflection of the quarrel, the confession from Barbara, and the team environment, she realized that Barbara had insecurities of her own and had not behaved poorly out of lack of respect but out of ignorance. As well, the group as a whole had come to the same conclusion and had decided to try their best to "forgive and forget." It was unfortunate that such an unpleasant incident had been necessary in order to better understand the underlying causes for the conflicts.

Chrys admired Barbara's strength and courage in facing the associates at the group meeting. The abuse Barbara received had been great, but she had handled it well and kept her promise to act as an active team participant. Although Chrys never befriended Barbara, as part of her loyalty to the group and to Japan Auto as a whole, she tried her best to support Barbara's needs as both an individual and a fellow associate. Moreover, in practicing her leadership skills, she acted as mentor when appropriate and kept constant check on her emotions, trying to understand and respond objectively at all times. One very important thing Chrys realized was that as a potential and effective manager at Japan Auto, she must not allow personal feelings to intrude on company objectives and, more importantly, associate morale and well-being.

Heart Attack

by Shauna Le Veque

On Sunday, November 28, 1993, 8:30 A.M., Shauna's father was rushed to the hospital because he was having a heart attack. Her entire family gathered at the hospital and waited to see what was going to happen. By the end of that night, her family went home because the doctors said that the test results weren't going to be ready until the morning, so everyone should go home and get some rest. If her father's status changed, the doctors would call the family immediately, but for now he was resting comfortably in intensive care. Shauna went back to her apartment and passed out on her couch from emotional exhaustion.

Monday morning at 7:30, Shauna called her mother to find out how her dad was doing, and her mother replied that she still hadn't heard from the doctors. Shauna expressed how worried she was about the condition of her father, and she wasn't sure if she should go to work or wait in her apartment for the news. Her mother told her that she should go to work, and as soon as any new information became available, she would page her. At 8:30 A.M. Shauna left for work. As soon as she arrived at work, her mother paged her with 911 after the home phone number. She immediately called her mother back, and found out that her father was going into the operating room in a few minutes to have angioplasty. Her mother told her to call her brother, and then for both of them to meet her at Cedars Sinai Hospital.

Shauna ran into her boss's office and told Mr. Hamid's what happened the day before, and that her father was now going into surgery. She informed him that she was leaving to be with her family at the hospital, but she would call him at home later that evening to let him know the outcome. If everything went well, she would come in the next day to make up the work. He said that he hoped everything was okay and to let him know if she needed anything.

History of ESD

Shauna started to work for Mr. Hamid in September 1993. Mr. Hamid placed an ad for a part-time bookkeeper at the local college. The ad requested that the person be experienced in accounts payable and receivable. The main position was to transfer information from his checking accounts into a new computer program, so his accountant could do the company's taxes on all his properties. He believed the data entry would take about two months. He also said that he wanted someone in the office to mind the phones and take care of other things.

Mr. Hamid owned ESD, a property management firm. He owned three large apartment complexes, with over 200 units in Santa Monica and West Hollywood, California. He also owned a strip mall with 15 shops in Sherman Oaks. Shauna had several years of experience in accounts payable and receivable, so when she applied for the position of a part-time bookkeeper, she knew that she had the qualifications to do an excellent job. Mr. Hamid offered her the job on the same day that she interviewed for it.

Mr. Hamid started the company shortly after his arrival in the United States. He had immigrated to the United States from Iran in 1972 at the age of 30. The first property that he bought was a small apartment complex in Santa Monica, and he quickly rebuilt the property by adding six additional apartments and expanding the parking structure. He then bought the West Hollywood apartment building in the 1980s, and found that to be extremely profitable. He and his wife did most of the bookkeeping, but when the company grew and needed expert help in the area of accounting, he hired an accounting firm. Mr. Hamid's wife continued to take care of the checking account, but when the accountant requested that ESD use a computer program for tax purposes, Mr. Hamid decided to hire someone for the position.

During the job interview, Mr. Hamid and Shauna talked about a wage. Mr. Hamid wanted to pay her $150 per week, but Shauna realized that if she accepted, she wouldn't be able to make as much money as she would have if she worked hourly. She agreed to work in the office Monday, Wednesday, and Friday, for seven hours each day, 21 hours a week at $10 an hour. That wage would only be for the first three months. Then Mr. Hamid would review her work and if all was fine, she would be given a raise to $11 an hour. She would also be entitled to some vacation, sick, and holiday benefits after she completed the standard probationary period of three months. They didn't discuss the terms of the benefits but Shauna figured that when the time was right, they would negotiate. But for now, $10 an hour was sufficient to live on. She was also getting a student loan from the government, and her father wrote her a check once a month for walking her parents' dog, and doing odd jobs for them, like grocery shopping and washing her mother's car.

Shauna had worked in various jobs since she was 16 years old, and she had never been fired from any job. When she changed jobs, she always gave her old company at least two weeks' notice before she left. Her only experience of a layoff was when one company transferred her department to another state, but they gave her six weeks' notice so she could find another job. When she accepted the position at ESD, she believed that she would be employed there until it was time to move on. She understood that as long as she performed her duties well, she would have a job.

At the main office, there were only three people, Mr. Hamid, his wife, and Shauna. Mr. Hamid's wife worked as the secretary and receptionist when her children were in school. But most of the time, the answering machine would pick up any phone calls, and each person had a private line with voice mail. If a manager from one of the properties needed to reach the main office, he or she would either use the private line, or call Mr. Hamid on his cellular phone. But if Mr. Hamid was out of the office and his wife didn't show up, Shauna was left alone. In the six weeks that she had been there, she was left alone more times than she worked with someone else.

During the weeks that she worked for Mr. Hamid, she never took any time off from work, nor did she ever show up late. When at work, Shauna felt Hamid was somewhat abrupt when communicating with her. He would give her an assignment without a please or thank you. He had a tendency to bark orders, rather than request it. However, Mr. Hamid gave Shauna a lot of positive feedback regarding her work, as well. She believed that he was sincere with the praises because she was quick and efficient. The week before her father had his heart attack, she finished entering all data into the new computer program, and Mr. Hamid was very pleased with Shauna's speed and accuracy. He told her that he was surprised that she finished all the entries earlier than expected, and on the Friday before the heart attack, he let her go home early. He even paid her for the full 21 hours that week.

Mr. Hamid's Reaction

At 7:00 P.M. on Monday, Shauna called her boss from her parents' home and informed him that the surgery went well, and that she would be at work at 9:00 A.M. the next morning. Mr. Hamid told her not to bother because she had proved to him that she was unreliable when she left the office that morning. She was fired. He stated that he couldn't trust her because she didn't give him any notice or ask permission to leave. All she did was barge into his office, state that she was leaving, and then she just left. She should have asked for his approval. Mr. Hamid stated he would allow her to pick up her paycheck and clean out her office the next day, but she had to do it between 3:00 and 4:00 because that was the time he was going to be there. He then hung up the phone.

Shauna's mother came into the room and asked her if everything was okay and she said, "No!" She said that she had to take the dog for a walk, and she would discuss what just happened later. She grabbed her cigarettes (though she was trying to quit) and walked up the street where she could see the sun setting over the San Fernando Valley. She found a large rock, sat down, lit a cigarette, and started crying.

Shauna was extremely confused. She was worried that her father might not survive his heart attack. She worried about how he was going to feel, knowing that his daughter was fired because she went to the hospital to be with him. Would this news cause more stress for her father, and would that cause another heart attack? The feeling of complete helplessness overwhelmed her. There was nothing she could do to relieve her fears of the possibility that she might lose her father.

She was also extremely angry that Mr. Hamid fired her without considering all that she was going through. How could he just fire her when she had been a good employee? Was it legal for him to fire her without any notice and for no good reason?

Shauna also felt relieved that she didn't have to work at ESD any longer. After she finished updating the books, she was bored at work. She had to ask Mr. Hamid for assignments to keep her occupied during her last week of working for ESD. She also didn't like Mr. Hamid, personally, because he had different views regarding work. He had stated to Shauna, on more than one occasion, that she should quit school and look for a husband to take care of her. "Someone who was as pretty as you would be a great catch, and you could make some guy really happy," he said. Even though others had told Shauna that her rich diversity of heritages, including Mexican, Indian, French, Irish, English, Polish, and Russian, resulted in a beautiful person, she thought it odd that he would make such a comment.

After sitting on the rock for an hour or so, Shauna gathered up the leash and walked back with the dog to her parents' home. She told her mother what had happened, and requested that they shouldn't tell her father about the firing. She was worried what the additional stress might do to him. Her mother agreed. She asked her mother if she could spend the night there because she was too tired to drive back to her apartment. Her mother was grateful to have the company, especially since her husband wasn't going to be released from the hospital for another week or so.

Tuesday, 9:00 A.M., Shauna went to the hospital to visit her father. She thought about not telling him that she was fired, but decided that he would feel left out, especially since this was important information. Her father had always been very supportive and at that moment, she needed the support. She told him what had happened. Her father said, "Well, it looks like you have to find another job. Do you need any money?" Shauna was very relieved that he didn't think it was a big deal, and that it wouldn't cause any more stress on him. She left the hospital and headed over to the office at 3:00 to pick up her belongings. She wasn't sure what Mr. Hamid was going to say, but she knew that she was going to confront him.

Confronting Mr. Hamid

She arrived at the office and found the front door open. She walked in to her old office with a box that she brought, and she began to place all of her personal items in the box. After she finished cleaning out her desk, she went into Mr. Hamid's office for her paycheck and to confront him. She was not asking to have her job back, but for him to listen to what she had to say. He just sat there while she told him that he was wrong to fire her just because she left the office to be with her family, while her father was having heart surgery. Since he did not react when she was speaking, she finally stated that if one of his daughters were ever in a car accident, and she were rushed to the hospital, he would certainly leave work to be there for his family. When she mentioned his daughters, he became irate. He told her that if he left his work each time there was some small emergency, he would not have been that successful. He worked many hours and many days to finish deals, and if he left every time to be with his family, he would not have as many properties. His face became red, and Shauna became a bit fearful. She realized that she and Mr. Hamid didn't share the same work ethic. After 15 minutes or so arguing about what happened, he stood up and yelled, "Get out of my office!" Shauna left his office relieved that she would never have to see him again.

Jenna's Kitchens, Inc.

by Craig Lundberg, Cornell University

Jenna's Kitchens Inc. was a rapidly growing, regional chain of family-style, franchised restaurants offering American and California-style, midpriced cuisine. Throughout the states of Washington, Oregon, Idaho, and the western parts of Montana, Jenna's Kitchens, with their "ranch-style" interiors (lots of plants, brass fixtures, rough boards, and gingham curtains), unique salad and dessert bars, and bakery sections, had enjoyed increasing customer acceptance. Typically situated on the major highways near the edge of the city or town, Jenna's Kitchens all had excellent parking and a distinctive, carefully maintained floral garden surrounding each restaurant. They were known as the cleanest restaurants of their type in the Pacific Northwest. The company purchased each property and built the restaurant, leasing it to the franchising owner-manager.

The success of the company was generally attributed in part to its technically competent buying and regional warehousing and distribution, but especially to unusual skill in negotiations with purveyors and bankers, and to a continuing "all-out" advertising program. Jenna's Kitchens had achieved some fame in Pacific Northwest business circles for its willingness to spend freely on manager and employee training, and on promotional activities, as well as for having only women in its managerial ranks. Over the years, profits had grown but by no means in proportion to the expanding scale of operations.

While the company paid salaries, wages, and benefits, in line with those of its competitors, many of its employees, franchisees, and district managers had been attracted away from them. Most members of Jenna's Kitchens regarded their jobs as desirable in comparison to similar restaurant jobs, and as carrying with them considerable prestige. Employee turnover in the restaurants and the whole company was low, and few people left of their own accord. While the company was not ruthless in its handling of inept employees, employee relations were, as one executive phrased it, "Firm. People take care to see their work is a bit better than satisfactory."

Jenna and the other women who had founded the company nearly 10 years before still retained positions in top management in the winter of 1990. The five regional managers, all women, who worked directly under this home-office group, as well as franchisees throughout the entire chain, frequently commented on Jenna's energy and enthusiasm. Her infectious aggressiveness and attention to detail were said to have permeated all parts of the chain.

The top management group determined corporate strategy and major policies, managed the company's finances, selected new outlets, and negotiated with new franchisees and suppliers. They delegated considerable authority in the actual operations of the company to the regional managers and gave some weight to their regional manager's views on broad policy matters.

Judi Singleton

During the two years she had been with Jenna's Kitchens, Judith ("Judi") Singleton, regional manager of the company's Inland Empire region (comprising eastern Washington and northern Idaho), attended many business meetings and not a few pep rallies at the home office in Portland, Oregon. Scarcely three weeks went by that she did not receive a personal visit from some executive from the head office. Judi Singleton usually used these visits to talk through some action she was planning on taking. Lately, however, no doubt because of the lingering recession these contacts had held what generally amounted to pressure for increasing sales volume and injunctions to keep expenses down. Singleton responded negatively to this pressure to cut costs and expressed herself openly, both to her superiors and to her own staff.

Jenna's, she asserted, was getting to be as bad as the large national restaurant chain where she had formerly been employed.

The Inland Empire regional office was located in one of the newer office buildings in the center of Spokane in the vicinity of the better hotels, shops, and theaters. It was considered a very nice location with many potential tenants waiting to lease in the area. The lease on this suite of offices was nearly $35,000 a year, and renewal of the lease, which was about to expire, would be at least $45,000. In addition, the regional office had several expensive direct telephone lines to the company's warehouse and shipping terminal. This facility, which consisted of a large warehouse with cold storage lockers, packaging equipment, mechanized revolving inventory systems, truck and railroad docks, and so on, was located in an area of light manufacturing firms, petroleum distributors, warehouses, and wholesale firms, all grouped together along the river a couple of miles to the east of downtown.

Moving the Regional Office

The top executives of the company had stated on several recent occasions that they thought Judi Singleton should move her regional office from the central, downtown location into a portion of the warehouse in order to reduce costs. Singleton had been clear in her opposition to moving the regional office, and top management, in accordance with its custom of giving authority to its regional managers and respecting their judgment, had been reluctant to force the issue. On a recent visit, however, the president, Jenna herself, had once again indicated what Singleton thought were very strong feelings about such a move. Singleton, finally, had agreed.

The warehouse had previously housed the regional office when the region was first established. After the downtown office suite was leased, the warehouse offices remained largely vacant, although still in a good state of repair. In anticipation of being reoccupied, Judi had the warehouse office totally repainted, soundproofed, carpeted, given new lighting, and otherwise renovated. At the beginning of April 1991, the 20 regional office employees and Judi Singleton moved into their new quarters.

Within a few weeks after the move to the warehouse, a noticeable unrest developed among the office personnel. Sensing this, Judi Singleton was seriously concerned. This new climate, in which lack of enthusiasm and strained relations were noticeable, was totally opposite from that which she had known during the past two years. All joking and kidding, in which the whole office had previously taken part, had disappeared; the performance of the whole office seemed lackluster and lethargic; even Singleton's direct reports had stiffened in their relations to her. For example, the inventory control manager frequently complained about being swamped with work and seemed always to be behind in his record keeping. The accountants and credit department personnel found it hard to keep up with their work and voluntarily began to shorten their lunch hour to resume work. In general, the work of the office was far behind the standard of promptness that had prevailed before.

The office workers' efforts not only reflected their attitude, but they continually complained about such things as the time they wasted in driving to work, about the noise and blowing dirt in the area, the inconvenience of having to bring their lunches to work or eat at nearby "greasy spoons," and they did not like to park in the warehouse lot among the pickup trucks and 4 x 4s of the all-male warehouse crews. Although no one in the office had actually quit, many had come to Judi requesting higher wages or had talked among themselves about finding better employment.

Judi Singleton thought about these complaints and the facts of the situation carefully, more than once discussing them with her husband. She discounted many of the complaints. She had made no changes in the organization structure or in personnel. All work-related procedures and systems were as before. The office equipment was the same. The jobs were substantially the same as before the move. Several jobs, in fact, had been simplified in that office members could now take up many problems directly and personally with the warehouse crews, whereas before they often had to spend a lot of time in lengthy telephone conversations or on inconvenient visits to the warehouse.

Judi Singleton believed that the refurbished offices, because of the carpeting and soundproofing, were not as noisy as the former ones. She remembered how the street noises, especially in the summer months, had welled up from the busy intersection that her office had overlooked. All office workers also now had free parking at the warehouse, whereas before they had to pay up to $80 a month for a parking space several blocks from the office. To avoid the rush hour congestion, the regional offices of Jenna's Kitchens now opened and closed a half-hour earlier than the warehouse crews and the surrounding industrial firms. Judi Singleton believed that, with this early closing, her office staff had at least an hour to shop or do errands in the city before stores closed. Singleton, along with some of the office staff, had her lunch at either June's Cafe or The Diner where the food was wholesome, well served and inexpensive, although the clutter of dishes, jukebox music, and truck driver chatter contrasted with the typical midtown restaurants.

Responding to the Complaints

The pressure for wage and salary increases, however, continued. Judi Singleton resisted for nearly three months because Jenna's not only paid competitive wages, but also because she was concerned that any increased salary costs might offset the savings from the move. Yet there was the felt risk of losing efficient, experienced people at a time when business was increasing, and competent personnel were still hard to find. As the morale of the office continued to deteriorate, and the pressure for wage increases mounted, Judi Singleton concluded there was no alternative but to raise the wages and salaries of the office personnel. Because she felt that the company shouldn't raise the wages of its office personnel without raising those of the warehouse crews, she proposed to the home office that an increase be granted to the whole regional organization. After considerable delay, the top management of Jenna's accepted Singleton's proposal.

After the increase was announced, there was very little talk in the office about wages and salaries. Instead, the office workers seemed to spend even more of their work day complaining about working conditions and about the "blankety-blank company." Morale continued to decline. The warehouse supervisor reported to Judi Singleton that the office situation was spreading to his crews, who had begun to talk about the company "going to the dogs." This surprised Judi and concerned her, since the warehouse crews had always been loyal and efficient. She also knew that, despite the recession, in the previous year, the sales and profits of Jenna's Kitchens had reached all-time highs. Her own bonus, reflecting regional earnings, was the largest of her career.

The penny-pinching of the head office disturbed her, especially after overhearing one of her managers say, "Jenna's is no longer pushing ahead. How can we be competitive with nothing but retrenchment? The company's about to go the way of all the rest of the big chains." Judi Singleton was disturbed. She couldn't move the offices back to downtown, and having just raised wages, Jenna's top management was not about to raise them again. Yet, something had to be done, and soon.

Julie's Call: Empowerment at Taco Bell

by Craig C. Lundberg, Cornell University

Glancing at her watch, Marcie saw that it was nearly 8:00 P.M. Conscious that Julie was going to call her in about half an hour, Marcie pushed aside her homework and reached for the file of her field notes (Appendix A) on Julie's store. Julie was going to want her ideas on empowerment, and she'd best get her thoughts sorted out.

Marcie Garner was a last-semester senior, majoring in hospitality management at Old Ivy University in upstate New York. Earlier that spring, anticipating a job offer from the Taco Bell Corporation, Marcie had approached one of her professors to talk about Taco Bell's newly initiated employee empowerment program—one of the reasons she had interviewed with Taco Bell. The professor wasn't very helpful to Marcie but did raise several questions about the program. While he and Marcie agreed that the idea of employee empowerment sounded good in general, they also wondered how easy it was to implement, and if it was actually working as designed. Marcie was encouraged to find out firsthand by visiting several Taco Bell stores and interviewing a sample of employees.

While she was quite busy finishing her program at Old Ivy, Marcie did telephone several Taco Bell managers in two nearby cities to try to arrange some visits. One of the managers contacted was Julie, the operations manager of the North Syracuse Taco Bell, who seemed at first reluctant to have Marcie visit, but finally agreed to a mutually convenient day in midsemester. On the appointed morning, Marcie drove to North Syracuse, met, and then interviewed Julie twice, as well as four of her employees each once, and was able to observe store activities for several hours. Near the end of the afternoon, just as Marcie was leaving, Julie approached her and said, "Your visit has made me think about whether I'm doing the right thing about our empowerment program. I'd like your thoughts. May I call you in a couple of weeks when you've had time to digest what you've learned here today?" Marcie agreed, gave Julie her telephone number, and they set a date and time for the call.

At 8:30, Marcie's telephone rang, interrupting her note reading. Answering with "Hello, this is Marcie speaking," she heard Julie's greeting, followed by, "I hope this is a good time to talk, Marcie. It's been quite a long day for me. Both Doug and Dan, you remember them; well, they gave me notice they're leaving next month, and now that spring has finally come, business is picking up. I've been jumping all day. I know you've been busy too, but have you had any thoughts about training and empowerment and such at my store?"

Appendix A

Field Notes: North Syracuse Taco Bell

Background

The Taco Bell is located in North Syracuse between two strip malls. It is a freestanding, brick and mortarstyle Taco Bell. There are a few other fast-food restaurants in the immediate area, including a Kentucky Fried Chicken. About two blocks away is a medium-sized mall, whose anchor store is TJ Maxx. Most of the other stores in the mall are also discount shops. The area looks a little rundown. My guess is that the building of the new and very large Carousel Mall, less than five minutes away, did not help this section of town.

The store opened last August, and everyone I spoke with was hired at that time. The empowerment program was discussed prior to opening the store (Julie heard about it at a training session during the summer). Employees have slowly been eased into taking on more and more responsibility.

There are four crew members and a manager or shift leader during slow times (one on the cash register, one on drive-thru, and two on the line). During peak hours there are four crew members on the line (two doing regular orders and two doing special requests).

People Interviewed

All of the employees are male, and the majority are in high school. However, the operations manager and assistant manager are both female. Julie is in her late twenties or early thirties. She was not wearing a uniform. Instead, she had on black pants and a short-sleeved blouse. She has been with Taco Bell for 3 1/2 years. Julie had previous supervisory experience as an assistant manager with McDonald's and with a franchised Kentucky Fried Chicken. However, when she came to Taco Bell she had to start as a crew member (line employee), because there were no management positions available. As soon as she started working, she was in training to be a shift manager. Julie works directly under Rob Robertson, who is a multiunit or "TMU" (team-managed unit) manager. Rob spends about one day a week in Julie's store. In addition to Rob and Julie, there is an assistant manager and a shift manager.

Darryl is presently training to be a shift manager. He is in his mid-twenties and has varied work experience. Besides working at Taco Bell, Darryl is a cook at a fine dining establishment.

All of the crew members who were interviewed have been with Taco Bell since the store opened in August. Doug is a high school senior. Previously he worked for Burger King. He often makes the schedules and is an "empowered" employee, so he can open the store without a manager being present. Dan is also a senior at the same school Doug attends. Before coming to Taco Bell, he was working for a family-owned fish and ice cream restaurant, and had some experience in telemarketing. His sales experience has led to his being put on a team that does OPS (off premise sales) calls. The third high school-aged worker is Floyd, who is a junior. This is his first job and he has not been given any additional duties but expects to be empowered this summer.

Julie on Taco Bell and Empowerment

"I first heard about empowerment at a training class I attended this past summer. At that time the concept was being called 'teaming.' I've never worked for a company that talked about letting line employees get involved in traditionally managerial functions. At the other fast-food restaurants I worked for, managers were instructed to be in control at all times. At Taco Bell, crew members are in charge of all kinds of things including preparing deposits, going to the bank, completing the closing paperwork, and opening the store in the morning."

"The employees of Taco Bell," Julie continued, "have much more freedom to think for themselves. They are encouraged to try to come up with something new instead of just being told how it has always been done. There is not one person who is in charge of making all of the decisions; everyone gets to contribute. The employees make more of the decisions. If they take action and make a decision, ultimately they will make the correct one and do the right thing. If they make a mistake, we'll help them fix it. What could they possibly do that we couldn't fix? Also, you don't have to ask permission for everything. Managers just say, go for it, and you don't stop."

"You have to be careful, though," Julie said. "It's not one day you're not empowered and then, voila, you are. It's a constant thing. There is always something to be learned at every level. Since there is always stuff to learn, I don't think a store can ever be totally empowered. There is constant training going on, and new people coming on."

"I think, overall," Julie went on, "the restaurant is better off because of empowerment. It lets the employees have ownership in the store. They will point to something and say, 'Hey, that needs to be cleaned,' or, 'It's slow, someone should go home.' That never would have happened at McDonalds. They have much more of an awareness of what's going on around them."

Julie said, "It really seems like the crew members are interested in learning more. Some of them are surprised when we tell them about stuff that we used to not be allowed to talk about to employees. In other places, they never were allowed to know the sales, food cost, or labor cost. It is nice, because they ask about it and they can get familiar with it. I think the reaction overall has been positive. Of course, there are some people who don't want any responsibility—they don't like empowerment. They just want to come into work, punch a cash register, and go home. Those people don't stay. If there is ever such a thing as total empowerment, those people won't be part of the team any more. They will be put out by other team members."

"Since we started really getting into this empowerment stuff," said Julie, "I think customer service has improved. Food cost is down and labor cost is beginning to come down too."

"If you are going to work at Taco Bell, you should know that people are capable of doing more than pushing buttons and sweeping floors. The biggest blockade to empowerment is management, who think employees can't do anything but push buttons. There still are some old-style managers who think this way. Really, they can do whatever you show them to do."

"Corporate is trying to teach these managers about empowerment. They gave all of us this packet on how empowerment is supposed to work. According to the packet, there are four levels of empowerment: (1) know what you are doing, (2) scheduling and stuff like that, (3) opening and closing the store, (4) doing everything without a manager. I think we are doing a little bit at each level, but not all of any. People need to go at their own pace. I knew most of the information in the packet already, but everything I read helps," she summed up.

Perceptions of Empowerment

Out of the 12 crew members at this Taco Bell, two are empowered. This means that those two employees have been trained to open and close the store without a manager being present. When asked what empowerment meant, the following answers were given:

Julie—"All the employees being self-sufficient in their jobs and having all aspects of the restaurant run as a team instead of the way it is traditionally."

Darryl—"Empowered employees can open or close the store."

Doug—"Letting employees open by themselves. Giving regular employees the power to run a shift. I opened the store without any managers and that's empowerment. Other places they wouldn't let you manage."

Dan—Had never heard the term empowered.

Floyd—"Being able to work by yourself without having a manager here with you. You're in charge that way."

Employees Speak about Empowerment

Darryl—"You get a little more money for being 'empowered' but not for doing scheduling or something like that. That is just for variety. Money does matter at some point."

Doug—"At Taco Bell you get a lot more responsibilities and privileges. At Burger King you only did one thing—I made the food but never worked the cash register. Here I've done everything.

There is more variety. I like it better here. Sometimes I like to see the financial statements too. You want it to do well, but you don't want it to get too busy. That isn't much fun. I would like to have some say in hiring. I think we'll get that soon."

Dan—"It used to be only the manager who made the schedule. When we started doing it, we saw how difficult it was. I understand the manager's job better now. I appreciate how difficult their job is. It's a little harder—I don't think I'd be able to do a lot of the stuff they do. I couldn't work the computer. They have to make the final decisions, like on inventory. Basically there is a lot of stuff I don't even know about with the computer. I'll stay away from the computer. I figure I'll probably never be manager (I'm not 18 yet). I'll just stay where I am. When you do that extra stuff you don't get paid any more. It is just something to learn. That's fine with me. The more I know, the longer I can stay here and the more hours I can get."

Floyd—"I look forward to coming to work. It's fun. We don't fool around, but it's fun working with your friends, and sometimes the managers will go out in the dining room to do something, and it's like you're in charge doing everything."

"I always thought that only a manager could do opening," Floyd continued. "That is why some of the crew members want to do it—so they could be like managers in a sense. This summer I am going to be empowered. This is something only Taco Bell does. It is something to work toward and look forward to. They show us the computer, or something like that, on a Sunday when it gets slow. They'll take us back there. It's nothing that big but it's something else you can do. It's a little higher."

"I think it is better if employees do the schedule," Floyd said. "It is easier to talk to them if you can't work a certain time. We all go to school together so you can just see them in the halls and let them know."

"Sometimes the managers go sit in the back," he went on. "They don't want to stoop down to being an employee that way—sweep or do the dishes or something like that. Everybody should be considered on the same level. It makes everything easier. Some people quit because they think the managers are better than them."

"This store could be run without managers with the people who are here. Sometimes you do. The managers will be in the office and someone will just take over. Maybe we couldn't do the computer work. But since they're showing us how to do it, we probably could if they just told us," he concluded.

Comments about Managerial Style

Julie—When asked about what her role as manager would be if employees continued to take on managerial duties, Julie seemed a little taken aback. Finally she replied, "I don't know. I never thought about it. That's a good question. Things change so quickly you don't have time to think about what your role is going to be. You just figure you'll free yourself up to do other things than working the line and saying, 'You do this and you do this.' We'll do community relations, and get new accounts. I'd like to have more time where I could get out from behind the line. Now I spend about 90 percent of my time on the line." Later in the day, after she had thought about the question a little longer, Julie stated, "My job is to teach them my job."

Darryl—"I won't ask anyone to do something I wouldn't do myself. So how could they complain? I am very fair. Also, I don't yell a lot. People like working on the shifts I lead because I'm easy on them. Also, if I have a good idea, I'll do things my way and show others that way. That makes it easy on everyone. I don't care how Corporate says we should do it."

Doug—"Over at the other place I worked, the managers didn't know what was going on. They would stay in the office. They weren't in touch with the employees. These managers do everything with us. They make food and help us out. These managers keep things in order, keep things moving along. Also, they keep us in line. Still, the managers are nicer here. They let us do more stuff and don't get mad at every little thing."

Dan—"This isn't very different from my previous job, except that being a corporation, they're not as mean to you. At the other place they used to yell a little more if things weren't done on time. Here, people only get yelled at when they are not doing their job. They'll say 'Do this' once, then 'Please do this,' and then they'll raise their voice. Overall, this job is more fun. I mean any job I got, at least I get paid, but I like the people, and the managers are nice. I got my friend to work here. I said, 'It's a good place to work. People are nice, and I can probably get you good hours.'"

Floyd—"The managers are nice and everybody who works here are friends. You can tell if someone's gonna leave real quick. Like if they didn't want to do the dishes, they aren't going to last. They have attitudes and get fired for talking back."

Customer Satisfaction

Employees are expected to do whatever they think is necessary to satisfy the customer. The crew has power to correct any problem a customer may have. For example, they can comp (provide free) food. However, sometimes customers want to see a manager. They feel that only a manager could solve their problem.

Dan described an incident when he had to go outside corporate regulations to satisfy a customer. "One time a woman came in and ordered a taco. She was from San Francisco, or somewhere in California, and said that there they come with olives for free. Here we charge for them. She was getting really mad, so I asked a manager. She said 'If that's how it is, then just give them to her' because, you know, total customer satisfaction. Make the customer happy at all costs. If they say you gave them the wrong change, you just give it to them, and you just tell the manager you might be over or under. You ask the manager first, I do, I don't know if you're supposed to, but I check everything with the manager so I don't get yelled at. If I hadn't asked, it probably would have been okay because the lady was getting upset and starting to raise her voice, demanding to see a manager."

Training

When new crew members are hired, they spend their first few days on the job shadowing another employee, or working on the line between two experienced employees. Julie would like to change the way training is allotted financially, so that new employees could complete a more comprehensive training program before they were expected to perform. Presently, the TACO (Totally Automated Computer Operations) system's Fast Labor program calculates how much time should be allotted to training, based on the volume of the store. For Julie's store it comes out to 45 minutes a day. Julie explained, "Well, a person is not going to work a 45-minute shift. Everyone moves at their own pace. You can't have a program that says that on day one, you should know this, this, and this. We don't have enough time for conventional one-on-one training. It's like 'We have time; let's do it now.' It'd be nice to be able to go step by step."

Due to the lack of training, turnover has been high. Recently, the training program was reevaluated, and some of the problems have been resolved. Julie explained how these changes came about: "The employees let the managers know that training was a problem, through roundtables with the training manager and the market manager. They had three of these discussions in one month and then never had one again—that was overkill. They had roundtables with two employees from each store, and at all three roundtables, the employees said that the training was not what they wanted it to be. So we looked at that, and said, "They're right' instead of getting upset and saying 'Who are they to say this?' We started to use the existing program more consistently. Trainers have to be certified to show they are qualified to train others. This program of certification came from Corporate. It was fine at first, but now I don't want to have a lot of different titles, because we're supposed to be a team and all on the same level. Having titles would defeat the purpose. So now if you're certified, you should know it well enough to show someone else."

Crew members have been very eager to learn new skills and take on new responsibilities. They report approaching a manager and asking to be taught how to complete a particular task. Every once in a while crew members will ask to take on something that management doesn't think they are ready for. For example, if crew members often call in sick, they are not ready to be in charge of opening the store. When this situation arises, Julie says she tells the employees honestly why she's not going to train them now, and that gives them incentive to improve. At other restaurants, the managers would just lie to the employees and say, 'I'll show you next week' and just keep pushing them off with no intention of ever training them. It's great to be able to be honest with them; they are surprised, and appreciate it. Then they'll try to improve so they can prove you wrong, and show you that they are ready to learn new responsibilities. In this way, training acts as an incentive."

Presently Julie is in the process of training the crew members to conduct employment interviews. For the first time, she has come up against a lot of resistance. "It is really scary for them. You can show them how to do a food order and they say, 'Okay, no problem, this is fun' or how to do the schedule and they say, 'Okay, no problem, this is fun.' But put them face to face and they're like, 'Don't leave me alone,'" she explained. To alleviate this fear she is letting them sit in on interviews she conducts. However, Julie cannot always coordinate her schedule and the interviewee's schedule when the crew member is working, and presently the need to hire people is overriding the need to train crew members.

Miscellaneous Comments

Darryl—When he becomes a manager, he says he'll have to cut his long hair. This came from the corporate policies. He thinks this is "ridiculous" because they hired him with long hair, and he can keep it as long as he's not a manager. Also, he says they make a distinction between men and women.

Julie—"We have more of a feeling of people working together than at other fast food restaurants, even from store to store. There are less rumors going around and people gossip less. You get more knowledge of the overall picture. Everybody gets to look at the overall picture, not just the RGM (regional general manager). You get to know where we are at with everything. It's not just, 'well, this is where we are and what we're going to do about it.' You look at where you are and decide what you are going to do about it. Whoever opens the store in the morning is the only one allowed in the safe until the shift changes. This means at times the manager has to ask permission of the employees."

La Cabaret

edited by Teri C. Tompkins

It was a cool Friday night in the summer of 1995 in San Francisco. Friday was date night, when most couples go out to enjoy themselves after a long week of school and work. A local restaurant was hosting "Comedy Night" that featured several black comedians. La Cabaret (the restaurant) was an average establishment, tucked away in the corner of a shopping plaza. The small parking lot was full of cars, and the predominately black crowd had begun to line up outside. A sign posted by the doors read "$10 cover, 2 drink minimum." People were grumbling about the high price as they made their way into the dimly lit restaurant. The chairs had been set up in messy rows around the stage and extended back until they met the tables and booths. At the left corner of the stage, Shelly, Malcolm, Betty, and Bob spotted a perfect table with a great view of the stage.

Shelly was a 22-year-old communications student at Cal Berkeley. Although Shelly was not born in Iran, she was raised in a household where Persian was primarily spoken and was very proud of her heritage. Her future aspiration was to attend graduate school and then work in mass media, although her path to this goal was not yet clear. Shelly was an idealistic person, very emotional, and generally well liked. Shelly had a relationship that she considered serious with her boyfriend Malcolm. They had been dating for two and a half years. Shelly was not sure where the relationship would lead, but she knew that Malcolm was extremely important to her.

Malcolm was a 29-year-old medical student of African American descent and was also extremely proud of his roots. He worked part time and juggled the rigorous course load of medical school simultaneously. In his spare time, he actively participated in functions sponsored by his black fraternity. Malcolm started dating Shelly in medical school, was very committed to her, and even had hopes of marriage sometime in the future. Malcolm was a very intelligent, easygoing person, with a kind heart.

Malcolm's long-time friends, Betty and Bob, were married and also African American. Betty was a graduate student in sociology, and Bob was an investment broker. Bob and Malcolm were best friends and belonged to the same black fraternity.

Plot

The two couples had situated themselves pretty close to the stage. While ordering their Midori Sours, Shelly examined her surroundings, and began to feel a bit out of place. While the audience at the comedy club the night of the incident was predominately African American, there was a scattering of Hispanic and European Americans. Their ages ranged from early 20s to 40s, and a majority of them seemed to belong to middle class families. Although she and Malcolm had been together for a while, she never felt comfortable when she was seemingly the only white person in the room. As the night progressed, comedians did their acts, often commenting on the crowd's cultural and gender differences. After several rounds of drinks, the crowd was rowdy, and a few audience members unsuccessfully tried to jeer back to the comedians.

The editor would like to thank the anonymous person who shared this very personal story.

You're Not Black!

The master of ceremonies came out on stage to introduce the next comedian, Harry. He had been featured on several cable and TV specials and was pretty well established in his career. "So, how y'all feeling out there?" asked Harry. He started off with a few jokes about "his woman" and a few sneering remarks about relationships. Due, in part, to their close proximity to the stage, Harry noticed that Shelly and Malcolm were an interracial couple. Harry turned toward them and asked Malcolm, "Is that your woman?"

Malcolm smiled and said, "Yes."

Harry replied," Boy, you've really searched, haven't you!" The crowd laughed as Harry turned to Shelly and asked," So, what are you?"

She replied meekly, "I'm Iranian."

Harry then turned to Malcolm and concluded, "You're not black!"

Instantly, Malcolm tensed up, his muscles tightened, and the expression on his face turned grim. Malcolm defensively proclaimed, "Let me show you how black I am!"

"Hold up, brother, relax now," Harry responded, while the crowd laughed.

Shelly turned to Malcolm and whispered, "Don't worry about it, hon."

From that point on, the focus of Harry's comedy routine was their interracial relationship. Harry mistakenly equated being Iranian with being Arabic and made derogatory remarks to Shelly about being a "camel jockey." Shelly tried hard to keep her dignity and class. It was very difficult for her; she felt like she stuck out like a sore thumb. It seemed like after each joke, the crowd howled louder and louder. Shelly felt like she was being crucified for the betrayal that some black women felt from their "brothers" who dated white women. She fought back the tears, fumbled with her drink, and wished she could just disappear.

Malcolm, on the other hand, was fuming. His body language screamed that he was ready to tear the comedian into shreds. However, not wanting to give the crowd the satisfaction, Shelly and Malcolm depended on their pride to sustain them while their hurt and anger increased.

Eventually, the routine came to an end, but the damage had been done. Shelly had difficulty looking her friends in the eye and felt very alone. She wondered what Bob and Betty were thinking. Why didn't Bob or Betty react? They did not seem to have been offended by the show, but would they have reacted differently if Shelly had been black?

Thoughts were racing through Shelly's mind. Should she confront the comedian? She wanted to explain to him that being Iranian had no relation to being Arabic. She wanted to know why a black man, who is so misunderstood in today's society, would make such false generalizations. She wanted to know why a comedian who had the power to influence people's perceptions would use his voice to perpetuate hate. She just wanted know why! Why, out of all of the "white" people, he had to pick on the one person who made the effort to understand.

Shelly tracked Harry down and asked if she could talk with him. Being an emotional person, she could not help herself; the tears came crashing down like a waterfall. Shelly was so overwhelmed that she could barely articulate her thoughts. All she could mutter was, "Can't we all get along?" Not one of her better moments, she realized. Malcolm rushed into the lobby and immediately confronted Harry. Malcolm looked as though he wanted to deck Harry, but Bob tried to intervene and pulled Harry aside to reason with him. At this time, Betty was nowhere to be found. Not wanting to embarrass herself more, Shelly pulled Malcolm out of the club, and they drove home. It was a long ride back to Malcolm's apartment. Malcolm continuously apologized to Shelly, knowing she felt humiliated, desperately trying to compensate for the awful night.

Moon Over E.R.

by Steven J. Maranville, University of Houston – Downtown,
and J. Andrew Morris

Six o'clock on a Sunday morning was an unusual time to find the executive administrator of Metropolitan Hospital, Inc. holding a problem-solving session with a head nurse. Nevertheless, Hamilton Bronson, executive administrator, and Edith Warner, head nurse in the emergency room (ER) during the previous shift, were finally sitting down to discuss the tragic event that had occurred several hours earlier. A patient had physically assaulted Katia Gore, an ER nurse, during her shift.

Because of the incident and the resulting turmoil, on top of the lean staffing and high demand in the ER, Nurse Warner had been in a frenzy, keeping the ER running as smoothly as could be expected. Now that Warner's shift was over, Bronson wanted to get the facts first-hand from her.

The Setting

Metropolitan Hospital, Inc. was a 500-bed, for-profit facility located in an urban sector of a major U.S. city. Metropolitan was recognized as one of a few dominant hospitals in a highly competitive market. The hospital and the market, though, had experienced profound changes in recent years.

During the early 1990s, the health care industry began a process of restructuring itself into a managed-care system. Previously, health care services had been paid for on a fee-for-service basis; insurance companies—or individuals receiving medical attention--would pay the going rate for health care services. Under the new managed-care system, health care providers entered into contractual agreements with health maintenance organizations (HMOs) to provide medical services for the HMO's members. The health care providers were compensated through a method known as capitation, by which health care providers received a specified annual amount for the care delivered to each HMO member—regardless of the number of visits or procedures performed. Consequently, health care providers were compelled to contain their costs to ensure the contractual relationship would be profitable.

Hospitalization had always been a major health care expense. Consequently, to lower their costs, health care providers avoided hospitalization for their patients, and when hospitalization was absolutely necessary, the length of hospital stays and the procedures performed were kept to a minimum.

This reduction in the demand for hospital services had a second-order effect on the operations of hospitals. Hospitals also had to contain costs to remain solvent. A leading source of cost containment had come through reorganizing and the downsizing or rightsizing of personnel. The health care industry was highly labor intensive and accounted for a vast amount of health care expense. Labor, though, was seen as being more variable than capital expenses in hospitals. Consequently, staff sizes in hospitals were reduced to achieve "optimal" productivity.

Sometimes, however, the lean operations of hospitals would come into conflict with patients' desires for responsiveness. ERs were quite vulnerable to these staffing issues. For example, as an urban hospital, Metropolitan's ER was frequently in high demand by those who were in need of critical, emergency care as well as by those who were without medical insurance or a primary-care physician.

The Incident

Nurse Warner looked pensive as she described the night's events to the hospital's executive administrator. "I remember Katia laughed when I told her last night's shift was going to be a nightmare. All the factors were right for an extremely busy shift. It was the second night of a three-day holiday weekend. The weather has been hot and steamy. And, as silly as it may seem, the moon was full. Unfortunately, my prediction was all too true. The waiting room was crowded from 10:00 p.m. on with patients and families. Most were having to wait over an hour to see a doctor since, of course, the most critical cases got first attention. The problem was there were so many critical cases and not nearly enough doctors or staff. Lately, with the move to managed care, staffing has been getting worse.

"Looking back, I should have done something sooner. Nobody wants to wait in the ER. Just after 2:00 a.m., a patient who had been waiting for over an hour started to become restless and rowdy. He demanded attention on several occasions, but his problem just wasn't that serious. I told him myself that he'd have to wait.

"As I was walking away, Katia came through the waiting area behind me. The patient leaped to his feet and demanded that Katia get him into the emergency room. Katia told the patient that more serious cases needed her attention. At that moment, the patient lost it. He was a large man about 40 years old. He grabbed Katia by the arm, threw her against the wall, and began swinging wildly at her, hitting her in the face and shoulders. People started screaming and running. The lounge was in a terrible commotion. Finally, the man was forced away by several other nurses and patients.

"The man was apprehended, but Katia was in pretty bad shape. So, we examined her and ran some tests. There don't appear to be any serious injuries. She's resting now in a recovery room on the fourth floor."

The Decision

Bronson wanted to act quickly before emotions at the hospital and in the community could get out of control. A violent encounter such as this one could have devastating implications for morale—not to mention the enormous expenses associated with the hospital's potential liability. Further, news of the incident could severely affect Metropolitan's image and market share.

Bronson commented, "We're used to the occasional squabbles between staff. We work in a high pressure setting. But, physical attacks—especially from patients—are quite different. Even though hospitals attend to patients who have sometimes been the victims of violence, hospitals shouldn't be the scenes of violence. Nurses can't be afraid to perform their work."

Bronson and Warner knew that, while this episode of violence caught them by surprise, the possibility of this type of violence occurring more frequently was growing. The hospital needed to take actions that would preempt—or at least protect its employees from—violent behavior.

No, Sir, Sergeant! (A)

by Joel Mitre

The tall, rangy sergeant stood face to face with his new boss, a thick and salty old veteran with over 22 years experience in the U.S. Army. As the hot New Mexico sun beat down on the two perspiring soldiers, Sergeant Mitre grimly glared at the seemingly calm Sergeant First Class Donald Fenceroy, the new ammunition platoon sergeant. He dwarfed his rail thin sergeant, and stared back, not knowing why Mitre hadn't yet responded to his lawful order. "I said, you need to have your soldiers rewash their vehicles, Sergeant." Sergeant Mitre was faced with a dilemma, whether or not to obey his new boss's order. By disobeying the order, Sergeant Mitre could receive harsh punishment, possibly resulting in a court martial and loss of his newly acquired rank. By obeying the order, Mitre would put his troops through undeserved stress, which would ultimately result in a severe loss of morale.

Charlie Battery, 1st Battalion, 14th Field Artillery multiple launching rocket system

Charlie Battery, 1st Battalion, 14th Field Artillery was in the business of providing artillery support to all units in the U.S. Armed Forces. Charlie Battery was a member of a multiple launching rocket system battalion, which consisted of four batteries. In the multiple launching rocket system were tank-like vehicles that had widely become known as the most powerful artillery weapons in the world. One multiple launching rocket system battery, which consisted of eight launchers, could level a city of 30,000 in a matter of two hours. By showering landscape with rockets and powerful missiles, a multiple launching rocket system produced a raining effect of baseball sized bombs over vast areas. A multiple launching rocket system battalion could efficiently destroy large circular areas in a matter of minutes. Thus, the term steel rain became the rocket system's nickname after its successful debut on the battlefield in the Arabian desert during Operation Desert Storm in 1991.

Charlie Battery, 1st Battalion, 14th Field Artillery was located in Fort Sill, Oklahoma, home of the field artillery. Each year this unit deployed on a major field exercise with its battalion to White Sands Missile Range, New Mexico, or Twenty-Nine Palms, California, for a 30-day-long war simulation exercise. In this case, Charlie Battery deployed to White Sands Missile Range, New Mexico. It was highly important to understand the stress involved with a deployment of this magnitude. Many of the soldiers were married and had children, and the month of separation takes its toll. The stress begins immediately and intensifies every minute thereafter. Thoughts of infidelity, sickness of a wife or children, financial difficulties, and countless other thoughts enter a soldier's mind. For single soldiers, often very young troops straight out of high school, the stress of having to perform under intense pressure causes severe morale challenges for their leaders. Additionally, this type of deployment means very little sleep. On the average, each troop gets about two to three hours per day, usually in the heat of a summer afternoon. Nighttime causes great stress because virtually all missions were conducted under the shroud of darkness. Each night troops could expect to run "balls-to-the-wall" from dusk to dawn, literally. Additionally, they faithfully believed that they would have time to pour a couple of canteens of water over their hot, aching bodies, in an attempt to wash away the grime and filth, but those times were more often than not used for highly desired slumber.

The team you will read about was an ammunition platoon within a multiple launching rocket system battery. Ammo's mission was to provide rocket and missile pods via the use of a heavy mobility truck and trailer ("Hemmet"). The Hemmet was a very large futuristic 8 x 8 truck capable of carrying eight pods of 48 rockets, or eight missiles. Two-man Ammo crews loaded and unloaded these pods with a large, tail-mounted crane. (I say "man" or "men" because women are nonexistent in multiple launching rocket system batteries). Each Ammo section consisted of a maximum of six heavy mobility truck and trailers (Hemmets) and 12 soldiers to man those trucks. In a nutshell, the section chief, usually an E-6 rank (known as staff sergeant), leads his section through its missions, which were directed from his platoon sergeant or platoon leader, by way of radio communication.

Ammo trucks were dispersed to deliver pods to grid locations, which correlated with grid coordinates on a military map.

Each team was expected to be able to read and plot grid locations on their maps, and create a route to that location. They must then safely transport ammo in a stealthy manner, often driving four to six hours in total darkness, using only their night vision goggles to see their way to the launcher reload point. Once they arrived at the launcher reload point, the two-man team unloaded the pods, which was strenuous work that lasted approximately one to two hours. Next they must park their long truck and trailer into a "hide" (a position where they are hidden) and drape a huge camouflage net over the truck and trailer, which takes an additional hour and a half, all in total darkness. Finally, the team could rest. They take turns guarding the pods, until a launcher arrives, and then they dismount the vehicle. While guarding the multiple launching rocket system, they download its spent pods and upload new ones. This takes about 30 minutes. When all of their pods have been taken, this whole process was reversed, until the truck was ready for its next mission. This process literally went on from dusk to dawn. For 30 straight days, this was the task of ammunition sections.

Sergeant Joel Mitre

Sergeant Joel Mitre was a relatively new noncommissioned officer, having been promoted just a couple of months prior to the deployment to White Sands. He would receive his first test as a noncommissioned officer—the war simulation exercise. He was in the process of completing his second enlistment in the U.S. Army. He was an unproven noncommissioned officer and leader to his supervisors, peers, and his soldiers. His leadership styles included a combination of delegation and participation. He was a firm believer that a noncommissioned officer's most important responsibility in leading troops was to take care of them. This was his primary focus as an noncommissioned officer. He believed he was responsible for caring for each of his 12 men's needs. Morale, well-being, training, direction of the mission, nutrition, sleep, division of work, communication, and protection were the primary aspects of Sergeant Mitre's objectives of leading his men. He was a personable and easygoing person with a positive outlook. He believed in mutual respect between himself and his troops and advocated the necessity of teamwork and being a team player all of the time. He often acted without considering the consequences of his actions.

Sergeant First Class Donald Fenceroy

Sergeant First Class Donald Fenceroy came to Charlie Battery from another unit on Fort Sill as a rehabilitative transfer. Although it was unclear why he was transferred, it was universally known that any soldier who was a rehab transfer had been in trouble in some capacity. Furthermore, it was a rare occurrence when a senior enlisted man was rehab transferred. Nevertheless, his arrival at Charlie Battery was preceded with a barrage of negative rumors about his harsh leadership style and incompetence in his job. He had over 22 years of service in the U.S. Army and had achieved the rank of a senior enlisted Sergeant First Class. He was a very quiet man, rarely showing emotion. His leadership style was autocratic. He simply told his subordinates what to do and they were to do it, no questions or thoughts about his orders were tolerated. Donald Fenceroy was a "by the book" noncommissioned officer. He appeared to be a solid noncommissioned officer with extensive knowledge of the chain of command and respect for rank. There was never to be any infractions on customs and courtesies with regard to rank. He had a high school diploma. Fenceroy was in his mid-40s.

First Sergeant Leonard Baker

"Top," as First Sergeant Baker was so affectionately known, was a highly respected first sergeant, and he was a Charlie Battery senior enlisted man. About the same age as Sergeant First Class Fenceroy, First Sergeant Baker was on the verge of retirement. As a matter of fact, this was to be his last field exercise. Leonard Baker was well respected by his soldiers because he was a man of his word. He did what he said and taught that same principle to each of his 100 soldiers. He was highly proficient in all of his duties, and had a correct answer to every question. Unlike Sergeant First Class Fenceroy, First Sergeant Baker had excelled in his 20+ years of service, having first been an ambitious student, a teacher, and a leader of men. First Sergeant Baker was liked within the battery because he empowered his noncommissioned officers with high levels of responsibilities.

Captain Dennis Small

The BC (battery commander) used to be a sergeant before becoming a commissioned officer. At 42 years old, Captain Small was slightly older than his counterparts. He possessed over 12 years of service, four of which were as an enlisted soldier. This was of great benefit, as Captain Small knew both sides (enlisted/officer) through practical experience. Captain Small was a noncommissioned officer at heart, and he backed his noncommissioned officers up 110 percent. There was zero tolerance when it came to disrespecting a noncommissioned officer. Therefore, Captain Small was well received by his enlisted personnel, and a sour apple among his young officers, who often felt like redheaded stepchildren. Dennis Small had a bachelor's degree in business and was the oldest bachelor in the battery.

Operation Blue Falcon

The loud whining of the powerful turbo-diesel engine could not prevent the exhausted sergeant from dozing on and off to sleep. His eyes, bloodshot and burning from lack of sleep, could see the objective was in sight. The bright sun warmed his cool skin after a long, cold desert night's work. His long body ached from the never-ending backbreaking work. His stomach growled loudly, demanding its first meal in two days. He couldn't help but think of his lovely wife and two children at home, whom he'd see in just a few days. He smiled, looking up at his five other trucks ahead of him. Sergeant Mitre had every reason to be proud. His 12-man team had accomplished every mission without a hitch, and distinguished themselves as the only section in the entire battalion with all six of its vehicles having completed the entire 30 day combat simulation without a single malfunction. This was unheard of in multiple launching rocket system battalions. He knew they were as beat as he was, knowing an AMMO Dog has the hardest and most strenuous job in the battalion.

The crisp smell of vegetation alerted Sergeant Mitre that the staging camp was near. The staging camp was located approximately 15 miles outside of the White Sands Missile Range. There was no doubt that every one of the 400+ battalion personnel were looking forward to it. After averaging two to three hours of sleep a night, often in the cabs of their vehicles, they would have the luxury of a soft bed and eight hours of sleep for the three nights they'd be there. Hot showers were a huge incentive too, as the majority of the soldiers hadn't showered in 30 straight days. The camp also provided a small store to buy cokes, candy, magazines, and so on, all of those items that were taken for granted the month prior. But, for the majority, there were phones at the new camp, giving them the long awaited chance to call home to their wives, girlfriends, and/or family members. There was no question that Sergeant Mitre had informed his soldiers of this camp, and after a month of living like animals, each of his troops was anticipating the new camp. Morale was higher than it had ever been.

Once the battalion convoy had successfully arrived at the staging camp, each vehicle had to be washed and prepped for the three-day drive back to Fort Sill, Oklahoma. By 2 P.M. the entire battalion had completed these tasks and retired to the many amenities afforded by the staging camp. Sergeant Mitre watched with satisfaction as his young troops eagerly went their separate ways. He felt great satisfaction that his soldiers were getting their reward for a job well done—"Sergeant Mitre!" Turning around Sergeant Mitre saw Sergeant First Class Fenceroy walking up to him. Mitre had known that Sergeant First Class Fenceroy was supposed to take over the platoon after their unit returned to Ft. Sill, and he wasn't looking forward to it. The many rumors about the rehab transfer brought about feelings of despair. As Sergeant Mitre inquisitively looked at the huge sergeant first class walking toward him, a look of near sadness captured Mitre's face. He assumed that someone had decided to give Sergeant First Class Fenceroy his new job a little earlier than was expected. "Yes, Sergeant," Sergeant Mitre responded. The tall black mammoth of a man calmly continued to walk up to his new sergeant, taking his time, and showing no emotion. "Sergeant Mitre, I inspected your trucks and you need to have your soldiers rewash them." It wasn't what Sergeant Mitre wanted to hear, but he didn't hesitate, "Yes, Sergeant," Mitre countered as quickly as Sergeant First Class Fenceroy's order had been given.

Sergeant Mitre hollered at one of his troops and instructed him to round up the section. As the young troop was getting the section together, Sergeant Mitre inspected his vehicles again. They looked good— in fact, better than the other vehicles in the battalion. In the distance, Sergeant First Class Fenceroy could be seen entering his air-conditioned barracks, which was heaven, inside from the scorching 100-degree weather. The more the tall sergeant looked around, the more the situation felt wrong. There was no one outside, everyone except himself and his section were relaxing. As his soldiers began arriving one by one, Sergeant Mitre went in to get the rest of his men, so that they could get this over with. His eyes nearly popped out of his head when he entered the barracks. Everyone was laughing, playing cards, chatting, and drinking Cokes. They'd all unpacked, showered, and changed their filthy clothes, except for Sergeant Mitre's Ammo Dogs, whose bags were still on the ground beneath their bunks, untouched. Fenceroy had just gotten out of the shower and sat with some mechanics to play hearts. Sergeant Mitre's face showed extreme disgust as he turned and walked out of the barracks.

The heat had sapped his men, but their trucks were very clean now and their chief, Sergeant Mitre, told his troops to disappear, which had a near literal meaning. Out of sight, out of mind, anticipating more B.S. from Fenceroy. As Sergeant Mitre returned to his barracks, he quickly got out of his fatigues and showered. As he did so he noticed Sergeant First Class Fenceroy heading back out to the Motorpool where his trucks were.

Once showered, Sergeant Mitre made his way over to the small store, which closed in 15 minutes, as he needed more cigarettes. From out of nowhere, Sergeant First Class Fenceroy appeared, with his usual calm facial expression and quietly spoke, "Sergeant Mitre, I thought I told you to have your men rewash your vehicles!"

Sergeant Mitre's brow furrowed, not really understanding what was going on here. "Uh, Sergeant, I had my men rewash the trucks and I inspected them."

Now a look of anger came over Sergeant First Class Fenceroy's face. He held his hand up as he cut off Sergeant Mitre, and said, "Sergeant, *I* inspect the vehicles, *I* will determine when they are clean! Do you understand me, sergeant?" It's not a good sign when a senior noncommissioned officer refers to a subordinate by just his rank; it is an unspoken fact that, in the Army, a soldier is on the verge of big trouble when he is referred to by just his rank.

Sergeant Mitre took a step back, looking bewildered, and replied, "I understand, Sergeant."

Again Sergeant First Class Fenceroy interrupted his young noncommissioned officer, and very slowly spoke as if to child, "Have your soldiers *rewash* the vehicles, Sergeant." By this time several soldiers had come out to see why good ol' Sergeant Mitre was getting his butt chewed.

Clearly Sergeant Mitre no longer looked intimidated; now he looked very, very angry. Sergeant Mitre stood in silence for a moment angrily staring at his new platoon sergeant. Mitre had only two choices, obey the lawful order, or disobey it. By disobeying the order, Sergeant Mitre could possibly be court martialed, lose his rank, and become confined. By obeying the order, he risked no legal action upon himself but would put his men through hell, lowering their morale to the point of no return. This would undoubtedly break them. They were being abused by their new platoon sergeant, and the whole battery was watching.

Sergeant First Class Fenceroy stepped closer peering down at the 6'3" sergeant, whose eyes displayed great dissatisfaction. "No," said Mitre.

Sergeant First Class Fenceroy looked stunned, that a punk E-5 buck sergeant would tell *him* NO! "Sergeant Mitre, I am a senior noncommissioned officer."

Sergeant Mitre knew where this was heading, a huge butt chewing. He turned and walked away.

"Sergeant Mitre, don't walk away from me when I am talking to you!" shouted Fenceroy.

But he didn't realize that Sergeant Mitre, too, was becoming extremely upset himself. To avoid further ramifications, Sergeant Mitre continued to walk to his first sergeant's room to discuss this with him.

"Sergeant! I gave you a direct order," shouted Fenceroy, trying to gain control of the situation.

It was at that moment that Sergeant Mitre spun around and began marching straight back at his platoon sergeant with purpose raising his hand, "No, you listen here Sergeant. I will be an E-1 before I *ever* work for you! Do you got that Sergeant?!"

Sergeant First Class Fenceroy's jaw dropped slightly—a reddish tint showing on his face. Sergeant Mitre turned while the stunned Fenceroy watched him walk away.

Rank Structures

Pay Grade	Enlisted	Abbreviation	Slang
E-1	Private	PVT	Private
E-2	Private 2	PV2	Private
E-3	Private First Class	PFC	PFC
E-4	Specialist	SPC	Specialist
E-4 (NCO)	Corporal	CPL	Corporal
E-5 (NCO)	Sergeant	SGT	Sergeant
E-6 (NCO)	Staff Sergeant	SSG	Sergeant
E-7 (NCO)	Sergeant First Class	SFC	Sergeant or "Smoke"
E-8 (NCO)	Master Sergeant	MSG	Sergeant
E-8 (NCO)	First Sergeant	1SG	Top
E-9 (NCO)	Sergeant Major	SGM	Sergeant Major
E-9 (NCO)	Command Sergeant	CSM	Sergeant Major
E-10 (NCO)	Command Sergeant Major of the Army	CSMA	CSMA

Pay Grade	Commissioned Officers	Abbreviation	Slang
O-1	Second Lieutenant	2LT	Butter Bar
O-2	First Lieutenant	1LT	Lewy
O-3	Captain	CPT	BC
O-4	Major	MAJ	Major
O-5	Lieutenant Colonel	LTC	Light Colonel or Old Man
O-6	Colonel	COL	Full-Bird Colonel
O-7	Brigadier General	BG	General
O-8	Major General	MG	General
O-9	Lieutenant General	LTG	General
O-10	General	GEN	General or Four Star
O-11	Commander-in-Chief (rare)	CINC	CINC

Authority Structure and Organization

C Battery, 1st Battalion, 14th Field Artillery (multiple launching rocket system)

<u>Type of Organization:</u> U.S. Army Field Artillery
<u>Size:</u> 100 personnel
<u>Purpose:</u> Provide artillery support for the U.S. Armed Forces

Chain of Command

       (O = commissioned officer, E = noncommissioned officer)

       Battery Commander (O-3)
       Executive Officer (O-2)
       First Sergeant (E-8), The "Top," First Sergeant Baker
       Platoon Leaders (O-1)
       Platoon Sergeants (E-7)
       Section Chiefs (E-6)

Ammunition Platoon Organization Chart

       Platoon leader: (O-2/1LT) Roger Conn
       Platoon Sergeant: (E-7/Sergeant First Class) Donald Fenceroy
            1st Ammunition Section
                Unnamed
            2nd Ammunition Section
                Chief: Sergeant/E-5 Joel Mitre
                Asst. Chief: SPC/E-4   Christopher Davis
                   Six trucks with two drivers each (Mitre and Davis included)

[Please do not read Case B until instructed to do so by your instructor.]

No, Sir, Sergeant! (B)

Sergeant Mitre knocked on his first sergeant's door. "Enter!" The first sergeant was getting up from his bed, and the battery commander sat on his bed, clearly they'd been discussing something. "Top" critically looked at Sergeant Mitre's face knowing something was wrong. Captain Small smiled at Sergeant Mitre, "Hey Mitre, what's wrong?"

For the next 10 minutes Sergeant Mitre ranted and raved over what had happened with Sergeant First Class Fenceroy, and finished up with, "First Sergeant, I refuse to work for that A—hole. I'll turn in my stripes before I do that!" The battalion chief and first sergeant periodically grinned at each other, as if they knew this was inevitable. First Sergeant Baker simply stood, "Sergeant Mitre, relax, go chill and let me deal with Sergeant Fenceroy, okay? Can you do that?"

Pearl Jam's Dispute with Ticketmaster

Anne T. Lawrence, San Jose State University[1]

The two witnesses raising their right hands to be sworn on June 30, 1994, seemed strikingly out of place in the wood-paneled chambers of the House of Representatives Government Operations Committee. Stone Gossard, guitarist for the popular Seattle-based alternative rock band Pearl Jam, was wearing velvet shorts, a loose pink shirt, and rope shoes. Jeff Ament, the band's bassist, was sporting pencil-thin trousers, a black leather jacket, and a backwards-facing Supersonics cap. "I am not used to doing this sort of thing," Gossard commented awkwardly as he began his testimony, "So bear with me if it's a little rough."

The grunge rock superstars had come to Washington to testify in support of the band's charges that Ticketmaster Corporation, the nation's premier ticket distribution company, was guilty of antitrust violations. In a formal complaint filed earlier with the Department of Justice, Pearl Jam had argued that Ticketmaster's exclusive contracts with many of the nation's biggest concert venues and promoters had given the company a virtual monopoly over ticket sales for many kinds of events. Ticketmaster had used its market power unfairly, the band charged, to drive up service charges, increasing the cost to concert-goers—including Pearl Jam's cash-strapped teenaged fans.

Waiting to testify later in the hearing was Frederic D. Rosen, Ticketmaster's feisty and blunt-spoken chief executive. Calling the band's charges "A work of fiction," Rosen maintained that Ticketmaster did not set the price of the tickets. "The acts determine their own price," he asserted. "We have nothing to do with that." His organization's convenience charges, he maintained, were fully justified by the service provided to customers.

The congressional hearing was just the latest salvo in what *Billboard* magazine called the "unusually public and freewheeling business dispute" between Pearl Jam and Ticketmaster. In June 1994, the dispute seemed rapidly to be spiraling out of both sides' control, threatening their reputations and ability to pursue their very different artistic and business objectives.

Ticketmaster, Inc.

Ticketmaster Corporation, the object of Pearl Jam's complaint, was the most successful ticket service company in the United States. Its corporate mission, in its CEO's words, was to provide "automated ticketing services to organizations that sponsor events in order to allow their customers the ability to purchase tickets to those events from outlets or over the telephone." In 1994, the company had 4,200 employees and outlets in 40 states, and processed over 38 million phone calls a year.

In 1994, Ticketmaster dominated the market for ticket sales to big name events at big venues. The company held exclusive contracts with about two-thirds of the nation's major stadiums, arenas, and amphitheaters—including such entertainment powerhouses as Madison Square Garden, the Meadowlands (New Jersey), the Great Western Forum (Los Angeles), the Boston Garden, and the Astrodome (Houston). It sold tickets on a nonexclusive basis for many other major venues. In 1993, Ticketmaster sold 55 million tickets, generating $191 million in revenue and a net profit of $7 million.

---

[1] An earlier version of this case was presented at the annual meeting of the Western Casewriters Association in March 1997. This case was prepared from publicly available sources and from materials provided by Pearl Jam and its attorneys, Ticketmaster Corporation, and the U.S. Department of Justice, solely for the purpose of stimulating student discussion. All events and individuals are real.
Copyright © 1998 by Anne T. Lawrence. All rights reserved.

Ticketmaster had not always been the market leader. In 1982, when Rosen took over leadership of the company, Ticketmaster had been a nearly moribund regional ticketing service owned by the Pritzker family of Chicago. At that time, the ticketing service industry was dominated by Ticketron. A subsidiary of Control Data Corporation, a mainframe computer manufacturer, Ticketron had built a successful business in the 1970s by selling box office computer equipment to arenas and stadiums and by providing off-site ticket sales, mainly at department stores.

Rosen's strategy for the upstart rival Ticketmaster was to provide superior, inexpensive ticketing services to venue owners based on a new generation of minicomputers. Rather than make money from selling computer hardware, he would make money from "convenience" charges to the customer. Rosen purchased inexpensive minicomputers and hired programmers to write software enabling them simultaneously to serve numerous telephone operators and sales outlets, such as record stores. "We were able to make a P.T. boat act like an aircraft carrier," Rosen's programming chief later commented.

Throughout the early and mid-1980s, Rosen aggressively wooed venue owners across the country, signing them to exclusive three-to-five year contracts to provide ticketing services. The advantages of Rosen's pitch to the venue owner were obvious. The venue owners did not need to purchase expensive computer hardware or worry about it breaking down. Someone else would handle ticket sales. Rosen also offered to rebate a share of service charges to venue owners—often up front at the time the contract was signed. And the cost of the system was largely borne by the customer, in the form of service charges added to the ticket price.

Throughout the 1980s, as it expanded its network of contracts with venues and promoters, Ticketmaster also acquired or entered into joint ventures with many of its regional rivals, such as TicketPro, Ticket World, and BASS. By the late 1980s, Ticketron was on the ropes, losing $2 million in 1989 and $7.5 million in 1990. In 1991, after efforts to find another buyer failed, the Justice Department approved the sale of Ticketron contracts (although not its computers) to Ticketmaster. Rosen's conquest of the industry was virtually complete.

In 1993, Seattle billionaire Paul G. Allen, co-founder of Microsoft Corporation, purchased an 80 percent share of Ticketmaster from the Pritzker family for $300 million. The Pritzkers retained 12 percent; the balance was owned by several individuals, including Rosen.

Pearl Jam

While Rosen was busy locking up contracts with major entertainment venues and promoters, the musicians who were to form his company's future nemesis, Pearl Jam, were beginning to make names for themselves in Seattle's fertile alternative rock scene of the late 1980s.

The Seattle music scene was in many ways unique. The city's geographical isolation from the rock industry capitals of New York and Los Angeles made it possible for a distinctive musical genre to emerge there. The city had its own network of clubs featuring alternative music, a progressive college radio station at Evergreen State College that favored independently produced cuts, and a shoestring alternative record label called Sub Pop. These factors helped support an unusually large number of innovative bands, including Nirvana, the first one to achieve significant commercial success.

Pearl Jam formed in 1990. In addition to Ament and Gossard, both veterans of the Seattle music underground, the band included lead vocalist and songwriter Eddie Vedder, percussionist Dave Abbruzzese, and guitarist Mike McCready. From the outset, the key figure in the band was the charismatic Eddie Vedder. The group's lead singer had an intense relationship with his youthful fans, with whom he strongly identified. Unlike many rock stars, he often wrote his fans personal letters, becoming—as he put it—"a part of their lives." Vedder was also more political than many of his grunge rock peers. He sported a tattoo of the insignia of Earth First!, a radical environmental organization, and over the years organized benefit concerts supporting abortion rights, international human rights, and youth voter registration, among other causes.

In spring 1991, Pearl Jam began playing club dates around Seattle, and almost immediately began attracting interest from major record companies. They eventually signed with Epic Records, a division of Sony. They released their first album, *Ten*, in August, and began touring in the United States in spring 1992.

The band's musical style combined elements of punk, classic rock, and blues. *Newsday* called Pearl Jam's music "a chaotic mix of muscular rhythms, piercing guitar hooks, and gut-wrenching lyrics." Part of the band's secret was its ability to cross over various formats. Cuts were played not only on "alternative rock" stations, but were also picked up by "heritage" or "classic rock" stations. In 1991, testifying to its crossover strength, the band won honors both for Favorite New Artist (Pop/Rock) and Favorite New Artist (Hard Rock) at the American Music Awards.

By the mid-1990s, Pearl Jam was being called the "hottest rock act" of the decade. Without a doubt, the band was a runaway commercial success. Although the band did not report its earnings, by 1996 it had sold over 17 million albums in the United States alone, and by one estimate as many as 30 million internationally. At the standard music industry rate of between $2.00 and $3.00 per "piece" for artist and songwriter royalties, the band might have made as much as $75 million on record sales alone—excluding revenue from tours, merchandising, and endorsements (several band members endorsed guitars and other products). Rosen was not off the mark when he pointedly remarked, as his dispute with Pearl Jam was being characterized as a David versus Goliath struggle, "They make more money than we do."

Although the band was extraordinarily successful, its members were apparently unmotivated by a desire for commercial success and appeared, in some instances, almost ignorant of the business aspects of their enterprise. At the congressional hearing in 1994, for example, the subcommittee chair asked band members their reaction to losing an estimated $2 million by canceling their summer 1994 tour. Ament replied, "I am not really sure how much money we forfeited. In a lot of cases the money at this point really isn't that important to us . . . [Making money] has never been our major goal."

The Dispute Heats Up

Almost as soon as Pearl Jam began to tour in 1992, it began to tangle with Ticketmaster. As a band that had burst on the scene to almost immediate mass popularity, Pearl Jam quickly learned that venues big enough to accommodate its legions of fans in many—or even most—cases had exclusive deals with Ticketmaster.

Troubles between the two organizations started with a few relatively minor skirmishes.

- In 1992, the band staged a free concert for its fans in a park in Seattle. For security reasons, attendance had to be limited to 30,000, requiring the distribution of tickets. Ticketmaster agreed to provide ticketing for $1.50 per ticket, angering the band—who did not want fans to have to pay at all. Ultimately, the city government handled the ticketing.
- In December 1993, the band scheduled a benefit concert at the Seattle Center Arena, with the proceeds to go to charity. Ticketmaster, which handled ticketing for the arena, initially agreed to the band's request that it donate a portion of its service charge receipts to charity but reneged just as the tickets were about to go on sale. After what the band's attorney called "a tense impasse," Ticketmaster finally agreed to make a contribution—although not at the level it had initially promised.
- In March 1994, the band asked Ticketmaster to disclose the service charge separately on the face of the ticket for a concert in Chicago. When the ticketer refused, Pearl Jam threatened to perform at another venue. Ticketmaster backed down, but said it would not necessarily agree to separate disclosure elsewhere.

After this incident, Pearl Jam began to experiment with alternative ticketing arrangements. In Detroit, the band attempted to distribute tickets through its fan club. Ticketmaster threatened the promoter, with whom it had an exclusive contract, with a lawsuit. In New York, the band tried to sell tickets over the radio; in this instance, Ticketmaster threatened a lawsuit against the venue owner. Pearl Jam later reported that during this period, Ticketmaster told the band's manager through third parties that they should "watch their backs" and threatened to sue the band if it interfered with the company's exclusive contracts.

Ticketmaster made it clear to venue owners and promoters that it would not tolerate any breach of its exclusivity contracts. In March 1994, the North American Concert Promoters Association, a trade group, sent a memo to its members—addressing them as "brother raccoons"—stating in part:

> Ticketmaster has indicated . . . that they will aggressively enforce their contracts with promoters and facilities. Ticketmaster's stance is that they have been loyal to their partners in this business and they hope and expect that their partners will reciprocate.

A subsequent update noted that the ticket service company "views the Pearl Jam issue as an all or nothing proposition, meaning that they will not agree to handle half of the available inventory on a show in any situation where a contract exists."

The Convenience Charge Issue

Against the background of these skirmishes, Pearl Jam began to organize its summer 1994 tour. The band decided to try to limit the price of tickets to its concerts to no more than $20, to accommodate the limited resources of their teenaged fans. To this end, the band priced their concert tickets at $18 and, through promoters, approached Ticketmaster with a proposal to limit its convenience charges to no more than 10 percent, or $1.80, per ticket. Gossard later explained that the band had "made a conscious decision that we do not want to put the price of our concerts out of the reach of our fans." The band also insisted that the service charge be listed separately on their tickets and that no paid advertisements appear on the reverse side.

Ticketmaster rejected the band's proposal, arguing that it would have lost money with a $1.80 service charge. The ticketer did make an indirect offer to the band, through intermediaries, to compromise on the issue. Rosen later explained:

> Various promoters spoke to the group—we had no direct contact with them—and told them we would compromise on this matter. We agreed to lower our service charges to $2.25 to $2.50, depending on the area.

The company refused to go lower, arguing that it "should not have to do something that essentially costs [the company] money just to resolve a conflict with a rock band." Pearl Jam refused this offer.

In mid-April, the band canceled its entire 1994 summer tour, citing the difficulties of touring without Ticketmaster. The band stated, "Ticketmaster has in essence dug its own grave on this issue. It is unwilling to be in step with the times and to cooperate with a band whose business ideals are commendable, given the state of the world today."

The Antitrust Complaint

On May 6, Pearl Jam's attorneys in the Los Angeles office of Sullivan & Cromwell filed a formal complaint against Ticketmaster with the Antitrust Division of the U.S. Department of Justice, at the band's request.

At the heart of Pearl Jam's antitrust complaint was the charge that Ticketmaster had "a virtually absolute monopoly on the distribution of tickets to concerts." The band and its attorneys charged that Ticketmaster had used "kickbacks" to promoters and venue owners to obtain exclusive contracts. The ticketer had then used its market domination illegally to push up service charges to "exorbitant" levels. The band's attorneys also charged that Ticketmaster's efforts to enforce its contracts with promoters and venues constituted a "group boycott," illegal under the Sherman Antitrust Act, that had the effect of preventing the band from using alternative methods of ticketing.

Ticketmaster defended itself vigorously against each of these allegations. With respect to the monopoly issue, the company pointed out that although it dominated the market for ticket sales for events at major stadiums, when all entertainment events were included, it controlled just 2 percent of the national ticket market. It faced competition from other ticketers in many regional markets; and the rise of new technologies (such as on-line ticketing) also posed a competitive threat to the company.

Its exclusive contracts with venue owners and promoters, Ticketmaster pointed out, were openly negotiated and subject to renewal every five years or so. Such arrangements were common in the industry; for example, arenas and stadiums typically signed exclusive deals with service providers for everything from parking to hot dog concessions. Up-front fees paid by the service provider to obtain these deals were widely used and in no way illegal.

Service charges were not excessive, Ticketmaster argued. Data provided by the company showed that in 1994, the average convenience fee per ticket was $3.15, representing 12.5 percent of the ticket price. The company claimed that its profit per ticket averaged less than 10 cents. Over the period 1990—1994, the service charge had increased on average 5.9 percent a year. Over the same period, ticket prices had increased at an average annual rate of 4.7 percent.

The company also stated that its charges were justified by the convenience provided. Customers were able to order tickets by phone, using a credit card, or at convenient outlets. They could obtain the "best available" seat, since inventory was centralized. Box office camp outs were virtually eliminated. Ticketmaster also provided information about events over the phone. In fact, the company reported that four of every five calls received in 1994 did not result in a sale at all; the customer had simply called for information, which was given for free.

Pearl Jam's attorneys responded that these assertions were "highly dubious, if not intentionally misleading." They stated:

> It is true that Ticketmaster operates in a narrow segment of the broad business of selling tickets to entertainment events in this country. Within that segment, however, Ticketmaster wields enormous clout by virtue of its exclusive dealing arrangements with venues and promoters.

The band's attorneys also called Ticketmaster's accounting figures, showing a profit of less than 10 cents a ticket, "ludicrous." Sullivan & Cromwell argued that this amount represented profit after deduction of large executive salaries, depreciation and amortization expenses that did not represent real cash outlays, and payments to venues and promoters to secure contracts. Sullivan & Cromwell also challenged the $3.15 average service charge, saying that Ticketmaster had distorted the figure by including charges on cheaper movie tickets.

Both sides in the antitrust dispute had their supporters. Representatives of several other bands, including R.E.M., Aerosmith, and the Nitty Gritty Dirt Band, testified before Congress in support of Pearl Jam's position. Several private parties, mostly Ticketmaster's competitors, filed their own antitrust lawsuits. Several consumer organizations—including Consumers Against Unfair Ticketing, U.S. Public Interest Research Group, and the Consumer Federation of America—also sided with the band. In several states, legislators introduced bills to limit service charges. Promoters and venue owners, however, generally backed Ticketmaster, citing satisfaction with the company's service.

Life Without Ticketmaster

As the Justice Department investigation dragged on, and several private lawsuits against Ticketmaster wended their way through the federal courts, Pearl Jam decided to go ahead and mount its 1995 summer tour without Ticketmaster, using alternative ticketing and venues not under contract with them.

In February 1995, while this tour was still in the planning stage, a music industry executive tried to arrange a meeting between Fred Rosen and Pearl Jam manager, Kelly Curtis. According to Ticketmaster's publicist, the band "crushed the mediation attempt." The band itself had no comment on this incident.

The band's effort to mount an independent tour was beset with difficulties from start to finish. "We'll do it," said band manager Curtis. "We've made our bed; now we'll sleep in it, " she said. "But it's a pain in the ass." Life without Ticketmaster required the band to play in nontraditional venues, work with nonestablished promoters, and use novice ticket distributors. The band's managers checked out parks, car race tracks, horse tracks, and soccer fields. But inadequate parking, poor sight lines, and security worries rendered most of them unsuitable.

The 1995 tour got off to a very rocky start. Several early concerts were canceled because of poor weather and security problems. On June 24, Vedder abruptly walked off stage mid-set in a concert in San Francisco's Golden Gate Park before 50,000 fans, saying he was ill with the stomach flu. The following day—little more than a week after its start—the band abruptly canceled the remaining dates on its scheduled eleven-city tour. Its publicist offered the following explanation:

> The cancellation was brought on by the business problems and controversies surrounding the band's attempt to schedule an alternative tour . . . [Pearl Jam] wanted to focus on its music, but instead has been faced with continued controversies associated with attempting to schedule and perform at alternative venues.

Tickets already sold for remaining shows were refunded.

Few other artists joined Pearl Jam's crusade. Although a number of other artists had supported the band's position in the Congressional hearings, none were willing to put the success of their tours on the line. Some observers concluded that Ticketmaster's apparent victory, in fact, had scared off other acts from trying to bypass the dominant ticketer. "[The dispute] showed how hard it is to tour outside the system. To mount a tour in the 'outback' is tough," said an executive of a regional ticketing company.

On July 5, 1995, the Justice Department issued a one-sentence press release, closing without comment its antitrust investigation of Ticketmaster, saying only that it did not have sufficient basis to bring charges. The department said it would continue to monitor competitive developments in the ticketing industry. Pearl Jam called the decision a "cave in." Ticketmaster issued a brief statement, saying that the action confirmed its belief that the antitrust charges "had no merit."

Ticketmaster had little further to say in public after the Justice Department announcement. The whole affair, however, may have softened Ticketmaster's unwillingness to negotiate service charges with top acts. For example, the company agreed to lower its service charge on Garth Brooks tickets, at his manager's request. But the dispute with Pearl Jam had clearly distracted the ticketer. In July 1995, Ticketmaster lost the huge contract to handle ticketing for the 1996 Summer Olympics to a joint venture between IBM and ProTix, a regional ticketer. Rosen said that Ticketmaster had been so "preoccupied" dealing with the antitrust investigation that it had not had time to address the Olympic Committee's concerns.

In the summer of 1996—shortly after a federal court in St. Louis dismissed the consolidated class-action lawsuit against Ticketmaster—Pearl Jam attempted once again to mount a tour without the ticketer. "We made a stand, and we're going to stick with it," Ament told the press. "Everything Ticketmaster stands for is what we're fighting against."

With a year's experience, things went a little more smoothly. But alternative ticketers used by the band were not always reliable, and many big markets—such as Boston—were bypassed entirely because of a lack of suitable venues. And ironically, even with the use of alternative ticketers, service charges were not much different from what Ticketmaster had offered in March 1994. Commented the editor of the concert trade magazine *Pollstar* of Pearl Jam's continuing crusade, "They're sacrificing millions by doing a tour this way. I don't see it having any impact on Ticketmaster, or anybody else but Pearl Jam."

References

All Things Considered [transcript of Public Radio broadcast], "Pearl Jam's Controversy with Ticketmaster Discussed," June 18, 1995.

Arnold, Gina, Route 666: On the Road to Nirvana, New York: St. Martin's Press, 1993.

Business Week, "Will Ticketmaster Get Scalped?" June 26, 1995.

Billboard, "New Set Pits Pearl Jam vs. Fame," October 16, 1993.

Billboard, "R.E.M. OKs Ticketmaster for Tour; Meanwhile, Pearl Jam Sticks to Guns," January 14, 1995.

Billboard, "How David Became the Industry's Goliath," July 9, 1994.

Billboard, "Play-by-Play Account of Pearl Jam Saga," July 8, 1995.

Billboard, "U.S. Drops Probe of Ticketing Business; Justice Department Finds No Fault; Ticketmaster Prevails," July 15, 1995.

Billboard, "Fans Sidelined by Flip Flops in Pearl Jam's Tour," July 8, 1995.

Charleston Gazette, "Creating a Stink Over Ticket Prices," July 28, 1994.

Consumer Reports, "Your Entertainment Dollars: Concert Tickets: Better Days Ahead?," August, 1995.

Contra Costa Times, "Pearl Jam's Ticketing Fiasco Deserves No Encore," October 8, 1995.

Daily Record, "Court Dismisses Antitrust Suit Against Ticketmaster," June 5, 1996.

Morrell, Brad, Pearl Jam: The Illustrated Biography, New York: Omnibus Press, 1993.

Newsday, "Sun Around the Bend," August 25, 1996.

Oakland Tribune, "Problems Force Pearl Jam to Cancel Its Tour," June 27, 1995.

Romanowski, Patricia, ed., The New Rolling Stone Encyclopedia of Rock and Roll, New York: Fireside Press, 1995.

St. Petersburg Times, "Getting a Charge Out of Tickets," [profile of Frederic Rosen], September 20, 1992.

St. Petersburg Times, "Pearl Jam Tickets on Sale by Phone Today," August 24, 1996

Sullivan & Cromwell, "Memorandum of Pearl Jam to the Antitrust Division of the United States Department of Justice Concerning Anticompetitive Actions Engaged in by Ticketmaster Holdings Group Ltd.," May 6, 1994.

Sullivan & Cromwell, "Supplemental Memorandum of Pearl Jam to the Antitrust Division of the United States Department of Justice Responding to Various Assertions Made by Ticketmaster Corporation," July 20, 1994.

Ticketmaster, Inc., "Facts About Ticketmaster and the Ticket Service Industry," n.d., approximately June, 1995.

USA Today, "Ticketmaster's Cyberfuture Is On-Line," March 10, 1995.

U.S. Department of Justice, "Antitrust Division Statement Regarding Ticketmaster Inquiry," [press release], July 5, 1995.

U.S. House of Representatives, Committee on Government Operations, Subcommittee on Information, Justice, Transportation, and Agriculture, "Pearl Jam's Antitrust Complaint: Questions About Concert, Sports, and Theater Handling Charges and Other Practices," June 30, 1994.

U.S. News and World Report, "Recording Sound Sales," September 25, 1995.

Wall Street Journal, "Ticketmaster's Mr. Tough Guy," November 6, 1994.

Washington Times, "Consumer Groups Go After Ticketmaster," March 22, 1995

Problems at Wukmier Home Electronics Warehouse (A)

by Kathleen Moldenhauer and Teri C. Tompkins, University of Redlands

It was late Thursday afternoon. Christi Titus, human resources manager for Wukmier Home Electronics, was walking to the office of Jose Garcia. Jose, supervisor of the finished goods warehouse of the company, had called her this morning to say there had been an emotional and heated exchange between two of the men at the warehouse. Jose had said he was concerned there would be a physical fight.

After Christi and Jose had greeted each other, Jose described what he had seen. "When I walked into the lunch area, I heard Manny yelling at Jim. He was shaking his finger and saying, 'You better just stay away from me.'"

"When Manny saw me," Jose continued, "he turned to me and said in Spanish, 'Keep this guy away from me. I don't want to see his face.' Then he stomped off."

"Something has to be done, Christi. There could have been a fight today and I don't want to see that happen. Manny was really angry, angrier than I've ever seen him. And you and I know how angry he can get."

Christi nodded her head. Manny had been known to lose his temper and after several years of observation, Christi had begun to form suspicions that drug abuse may have exacerbated his outbursts.

"Do you mind if I use your office to interview Manny and Jim?" Christi asked.

"No, no, go right ahead, " Jose answered. "I have some work to do out there right now anyway."

The Angry Lunch Encounter

Christi decided that she need to meet individually with each man and hear his side of the story. She called Manny to the office first. Christi had known him for the five years that she had worked for Wukmier.

As soon as he sat down, he said, "You've got to do something about Jim. I've tried to talk to the guy; I've tried to tell him to mind his own business and just do the work, but this guy, Jim, will not listen."

Manny stood and began pacing the floor looking angry as he continued, "Jim complains about the music we play. We've played Spanish music for a long time, long before Jim. Last week Jim brought his own radio. He was playing it very loud. Jose told him to turn it down. Jim asked why he had to turn his radio down, but no one else did. Then Jose told us there were no more radios allowed. Everyone had to take his radio home. Jim ruined it for all of us."

Christi asked about what happened in the morning.

Manny explained that one of the other guys, Pete, was eating his lunch, and Jim had made a comment about Manny. "When Pete told me what Jim said, I went over to Jim and told him, 'I don't want you talking about me. I don't want you in my business. Just do your work and stay away from me.'" Manny said about that time Jose appeared. Manny said to Jose, "I have told you before, keep this guy away from me."

"What did he say that was so upsetting?" Christi asked.

"It's not important what he said. He just made a rude comment about me. I just don't want this guy in my business."

After several more attempts to find out what Jim had said, Christi told Manny that she would be conducting an investigation for the company and, after talking to several employees, would get back with him as soon as possible.

Next Jim was summoned. Christi asked him what had occurred that morning. "I was passing through the lunch area where Pete was having lunch. He was having some soup. He also had several small packages with condiments wrapped in foil. I jokingly said, 'You better not let Manny see that parsley because he will want it.' A short time later Manny confronted me and he looked very angry. He was yelling and told me to stay away from him and to stay out of his business. When our supervisor, Jose, appeared, Manny started yelling at him but I don't know what he was saying because he was yelling in Spanish."

"Did you feel threatened by Manny?" Christi asked.

"Yes, he asked me if I wanted to go outside. I didn't want to fight because I don't want to lose my job. I was working out in an area where I was alone. He was very mad. He told me I better watch my back. I'm afraid he might do something."

"Why did you make the comment that Manny would want Pete's lunch?"

"I was just joking around," Jim replied.

Christi looked at Jim puzzled. "Why would a comment about parsley cause Manny to be so angry?" she wondered.

Jim shrugged his shoulders and looked away. After a few more questions, Christi told Jim that she would get back with him as soon as possible.

Pete was next to be interviewed. He confirmed what Jim had said regarding his lunch. When asked why Jim made the statement about his lunch, Pete said he did not know.

"What were you eating?" Christi asked.

"I was having some Menudo soup and some condiments wrapped in foil," Pete replied.

"What were the condiments?"

"Tortillas along with chopped onion, tomato, and parsley."

"Did you tell Manny what Jim had said about the parsley?"

Pete looked nervous, "Yeah, but I didn't know it would upset him. I thought they had patched things up. I saw them laughing and talking together a few days before."

As Christi talked to Pete, she remembered that marijuana was sometimes wrapped in foil. Some types of drugs were smoked using parsley. She wondered if this was the basis of Jim's "joke," so she asked Pete if he was aware of Manny smoking marijuana, either at work or away from work.

"No, why would I know?" Pete said looking away and rubbing his hand against his trousers several times. It appeared to Christi that this line of questioning made Pete very nervous.

In talking to two other employees who were in the vicinity, both said they did not see or hear the argument. One of the men was in the lunch area and did hear the comment made by Jim. When he was asked about the comment, he too said that he didn't know why it was made. When he was asked about any use of marijuana by employees of the warehouse, he said he did not know. He too appeared uncomfortable.

The Finished Goods Warehouse

The finished goods warehouse was an old building that was open across the front with six truck bays. The cement floor was dirty from the forklifts, trucks delivering and picking up products, and dust from the street traffic. The warehouse held finished goods from Wukmier's manufacturing plant located about three miles away. The company manufactured an expensive line of home electronics, and racks with boxes of products were spread throughout the warehouse. The finished goods warehouse was the staging area from which products were shipped to other parts of the country. Lighting in the warehouse had been added over the years, but there was still a dark feeling about the areas beyond the open bays.

When Christi had arrived to investigate the lunch incident, she saw the traffic clerk in his office, which was centrally located about 100 feet inside the open bay area. Security cameras, monitored by the staff at the manufacturing plant, were placed in strategic locations in the building. Christi had walked to Jose's office, which was located in the back. A warehouse employee sat at his table near the staging area writing an order. He had looked up and nodded, but did not smile. This was understandable since, with only nine employees, everyone was aware of the morning incident.

There were seven warehouse employees, a traffic clerk, and the warehouse supervisor located at the finished goods warehouse. Eight of these employees had worked together for many years. Until nine months ago, the employees who worked at the finished goods warehouse had been at the warehouse from eight to thirty years. All of them were of Mexican heritage, half of them first generation immigrants, and the other half, second generation. Most lived within a five-mile radius of the facility. The local area was populated primarily by Hispanics. Employees of the warehouse believed their job was important. Attendance was very good and turnover was non-existent. Employees at the finished goods warehouse belonged to a union. Grievance, promotion, and termination procedures were specified in the contract with the union.

None of the employees received formal job training except for a once a year safety course. They learned their job by observation and coaching from the seasoned employees. Although forklift trucks were used to move products in and out of inventory, there were also some physical aspects to the job. At times, a person needed to hand-load a trailer, lifting and moving numerous 50-pound boxes, or a couple of people were needed to move around a 300-pound package. The work was very routine, consisting of receiving orders, pulling the product from inventory, staging the order (setting it up by the truck bay), writing it up, and then loading it on to a trailer.

Benefits for employees included medical insurance provided by an HMO type of carrier. When needed, the Wukmier's human resource professionals utilized the services of an employee assistance program (EAP) when they wanted an outside professional opinion or to provide resources to employees and their families during times of crisis, grief, loss, or abuse. In conjunction with the employees' medical carrier, professionals from the employee assistance program could arrange for employee support such as psychiatric care and counseling or smoking cessation programs.

Jose and Christi

Jose and Christi had been working together for five years, since Christi had joined Wukmier. Christi had a degree in management and human resources. Employees respected Christi because she visited them regularly, and because she knew most of the company's 425 employees by name. Christi's previous work experience included several years in a school district including five years working in a high school dean's office. There, she had gained a lot of experience dealing with interpersonal behavior, diversity issues, and drug and alcohol abuse problems. Christi was 45 years old and Caucasian. She had grown up in a culturally diverse neighborhood within 25 miles of the warehouse.

Jose Garcia, the 48 year-old warehouse supervisor, had been with the company for over 30 years. He had started out as a warehouse employee and had been warehouse supervisor for over 10 years. Jose had no formal education; his skills had been entirely learned on the job. He immigrated to the United States from Mexico when he was about 16 years old. While he communicated in English well, he had a heavy accent and felt uncomfortable with his language skills. He was a hard working employee and very direct in his communication with subordinates. Christi believed Jose used an authoritarian style of supervision. He set expectations for daily quotas of released shipments and made assignments to each employee. Although Jose was blunt and straightforward when he directed the workers in their tasks, he didn't separate himself from his employees. He worked right along with them, often driving a forklift and helping move product to meet their daily quota of shipments. The workers had told Christi that they felt they were able to influence Jose. They liked the fact that he allowed them to listen to music while working, that he gave them freedom to use the telephone, and that he made sure that they took turns doing the various tasks required at work.

Manny and Jim

Manny had worked as a warehouse employee for Wukmier for 17 years. It was his first job out of high school. He was married and had two children. Manny was the union shop steward. Christi assessed him as an average performer. Manny's moods were somewhat unpredictable; he could be moody and had had disagreements with a couple of his co-workers. While his number of absences were not excessive, he tended to miss Mondays the most often. Rumor was that he liked to party and sometimes couldn't make it in after a weekend. He had previously complained to Christi about Jose yelling at him and he had complained about Jim. Generally, however, he got along with his coworkers. Manny was in his mid- to late thirties. He was Mexican, a high school graduate, who grew up in a nearby neighborhood populated primarily by Hispanics.

The other employee, Jim, had worked with the company for nine months; he held the first new position in years that had been added to the finished goods warehouse. Christi and Jose had hired him after advertising the position and interviewing several good candidates. Jim looked the most promising with about four years of previous warehouse experience. He was Caucasian, age 26, a high school graduate, and grew up in a suburban area in a middle-income neighborhood. He had been in recovery from drug and alcohol abuse, had been sober for about two years, and regularly attended support meetings. Because of his previous work experience, Jim felt confident about his work. The supervisor and the other employees agreed that he was a fast worker.

In the nine months that Jim had been with Wukmier, Christi had had several previous encounters with him or about him. Jim had complained to his supervisor, to his fellow employees, and to Christi about the Latin music that was played daily at the warehouse. He said that they should listen to different types of music. He stated that it was not a racial thing. He said he was not prejudiced; he had worked with all types of people. He just did not want to listen to Latin music all the time at work.

Another concern about Jim came from his fellow employees. The method of moving material had evolved over time and everyone in the warehouse accepted it as the right way to do things. Jim had been trained by another method and he thought his way was just as effective and safe. When employees at Wukmier tried to get him to load their way, Jim ignored them. When they complained to Jose, he didn't make Jim change his method. Some employees felt that he treated Jim differently than the rest of them. Hadn't he insisted that they load material the Wukmier way before Jim arrived? Why was Jim allowed to ignore standard procedure?

Christi found that the long-term employees were united when it came to their concern about the newcomer. Jim said he didn't understand what the problem was. He felt that he did his job well, working quickly to pull his orders. He felt successful in his previous job and expected to be successful in this one. He seemed unconcerned about the other employees' complaints about him. Christi had held several meetings with individuals and then a group meeting. The meetings seemed to resolve the extreme emotions, but only for a short period of time.

Christi also knew that Jim had recently bought a new car and that Manny had purchased Jim's old car. As far as she knew, the deal had been satisfactory to both of the men.

The Decision

Now Christi needed to make a decision about what to do. She stood up and walked into the warehouse looking for Jose. He was standing by one of the open bays. He saw her and walked back toward her and his office.

"Jose," she said quietly, " Let's go back into your office. I'll tell you what I've found out and then we need to make a decision about what to do."

[Please do not read Part B until instructed to do so by your instructor.]

Problems at Wukmier Home Electronics Warehouse (B)

Jose Garcia and Christi Titus talked about what Christi had found during her conversations with the employees. Jose said he had no knowledge of marijuana use, but he did remember an incident of about eight years prior. The police had stopped Manny and another employee out in front of the building during a lunch break. There was a question about whether they were smoking marijuana. Christi told Jose that she suspected that Manny might have a drug problem. She also told him that she was concerned that he had an anger management problem. In addition, she felt Jim was not trying very hard to fit in with the rest of the employees.

Christi thought about what her options were regarding Manny and Jim. She had always practiced a policy of zero tolerance for violence or the threat of violence. She wanted to resolve the problem so everyone could be productive at work.

✓ She could suspend Manny with no pay for a period of time. She wondered if that would be effective in communicating to Manny that threats were not acceptable at work. She could also use the suspension to allow time to gather additional information. A decision could be made after an investigation of whether to terminate or not.

✓ She could terminate Manny. Did she have sufficient cause to terminate him? How would that affect the other employees?

✓ She could suspend Jim. She wondered if she had sufficient cause to suspend him.

✓ She could refer Manny and/or Jim to the employee assistance program for evaluation. The EAP policy stated that an employee's file was confidential. If she wanted information on Manny or Jim, the employee would have to sign a release allowing Christi to discuss the case with the EAP counselor.

✓ She could request that Manny take a drug test. By union rules, Wukmier was allowed to take random tests or, if they had an employee's written permission, they could ask a specific employee to take a drug test. The employee had the right to refuse.

✓ She could request that Manny enroll in an anger management course. She knew that the employee assistance program (EAP) could make the arrangements for enrollment. She wasn't sure that Manny would be willing to take the course, however.

✓ She could choose a combination of the options.

After a short conversation with Jose, Christi made her decision, and called first Manny and then Jim into the office to inform them.

Questions Matter!

by Cathy Paul

Cathy Parker was excited as she made her early morning, 15 minute, commute to work to her new job at EBSCO Subscription Services. Her two-hour drive to her former job was history. Cathy's new job also provided her with medical, dental, and retirement benefits that were not offered to her at her previous job, due to her temporary status. She even laughed to herself as she thought about having her own computer, desk, and phone. These items, to some, may have seemed trivial, but at her last job, she spent six years being shifted around from one desk to another, based on the work demand.

EBSCO Subscriptions Services

Her new position, customer service representative, was at the Los Angeles regional office of EBSCO Subscription Services (ESS). As a single-source subscription provider, ESS minimized costs and maintained efficiency by facilitating the subscription process to thousands of journals. ESS offered libraries and institutions a convenience. They placed their orders through EBSCO, received the invoice, and wrote one check for most of their subscriptions, such as print, CD-ROM, and electronic journals. Almost any periodical published, domestic and international, could be ordered through ESS. An international network of offices located in 21 countries enhanced worldwide service. Some of these countries included Australia, Canada, Germany, Malaysia, and Taiwan. Nine regional offices, strategically located, to provide personalized, effective service, supported customers in the United States. All offices were linked together electronically and worked closely together to ensure customer satisfaction.

The Los Angeles regional office was comprised of approximately 40 employees, including the regional manager. The office staff was ethnically diverse, including Chinese, Japanese, Caucasian, Samoan, and African American workers. The office was predominately female and had only three male employees. The customer service departments were segregated into three areas: schools and universities, corporate accounts, and hospitals and medical libraries.

Cathy's Training

Cathy began her training in the schools and universities department, under the direct supervision of Julie Trenton, customer service supervisor. Cathy felt comfortable working with Julie, as she found her easygoing. Julie reinforced that she had an open door policy, should any questions or concerns arise. Julie was a single female in her early forties, as was Cathy, and Cathy soon discovered that they had a lot in common because they had both grown up on the South Bay, had gone to neighboring high schools, and coincidentally, knew many of the same people.

Although the training, at times, was extremely detail oriented, Julie felt that Cathy caught on quickly and, after three weeks of training, left her to work on her own. Cathy was proud of this accomplishment, for she had always prided herself on working independently with minimum supervision. After working two months in the schools and universities customer service department, Cathy was promoted to the position of customer service support for the hospital and medical libraries department.

Her duties included backup support for the other three members of the department. This included Fay Hill, age 50, a 20-year employee of ESS. Fay was very soft-spoken and mostly kept to herself. Cathy was informed by Julie that Fay liked to be in control of her own work, and was very hesitant to allow someone to assist her. Cathy took this into consideration, but eventually approached Fay, and asked if there was any work that she could help her with. After a few weeks, in which she politely declined her offers to help, Fay, finally, did allow Cathy to assist her, when she typed some correspondence letters to publishers. Cathy also filed claims for missing issues for Los Angeles County/USC Medical Center, one of Fay's biggest accounts. Cathy ensured that Fay was kept abreast of the status of the claims and her contact with various publishers as she helped to get problems resolved.

Cathy also worked with Sharon Davis, age 26, who had been with ESS for 18 months. Sharon's bubbly personality made her very approachable, and Cathy soon discovered that, although Sharon hadn't been with the company long, she was extremely knowledgeable when it came to solving problems with accounts. Cathy found Sharon to be a valuable resource when questions arose.

The third member of the department, Beverly Thomas, age 62, also a 20-year employee with the company, was the one member of the department with whom Cathy worked most closely. The number of accounts that Beverly handled had grown rapidly prior to Cathy joining the department, and it had been determined that Cathy would take over some of Beverly's responsibilities. Cathy answered Beverly's daily correspondence, assisted with return phone calls to publishers and customers, and entered publishers' replies to claims in the computer system. Cathy found Beverly to be very patient when asked a question (even if it was asked more than once) and was pleased with how Beverly constantly reminded her of how much her help and work were appreciated.

New Supervisor

Everything, at that point, had gone well and ran smoothly, when, ten weeks after Cathy started with ESS, an urgent staff meeting was called. It was announced at the meeting that the group's immediate supervisor, Julie Trenton, was leaving ESS to accept a position with the American Honda Company. Cathy and her fellow employees were saddened when they heard the news. They had built a good working relationship with Julie, and she was well respected and trusted.

It was announced that Amanda Holt would be the new supervisor, which caught everyone by surprise. Amanda, age 40, had been an accountant with the company for nine years but had never managed people before. But discussion among employees came to the conclusion that they would give Amanda the benefit of the doubt, and that time would prove to be the best indicator of her management skills.

It wasn't long before Cathy realized that Amanda's way of managing employees greatly differed from that of her predecessor, Julie. Shortly after Amanda began her new supervisory position, she called Cathy into her office. With the explanation that she wanted to understand the work that Cathy was doing and help her to do it better, she proceeded by telling her how the dynamics of her workday were now going to change.

Ask No Questions

Effective immediately, Cathy could not ask questions of the coworkers within her department; all questions were to be directed to Amanda. This led to feelings of anger and frustration for Cathy, because she questioned Amanda's lack of familiarity with the hospital and medical libraries department, specifically, its customers that Cathy dealt with on a daily basis. Cathy also felt that because Beverly Thomas had ten years more experience with the company than Amanda, Beverly should be the source to answer questions. Amanda also instructed Cathy to save all of her daily work. Every afternoon, Amanda would go over the work with Cathy and addressed any corrections needed. When Cathy explained to Amanda that she was accustomed to working independently, with minimum supervision, Amanda rebutted that she was not "out to get her" and justified her actions as trying to help Cathy understand her job better. However, Cathy believed that Amanda singled her out for some reason and wondered if this was a "power trip," or if Amanda's intimidating management techniques would continue indefinitely.

Cathy wanted Amanda to create an open communication environment during discussions. Cathy felt that their conversations were one-sided. Amanda interrupted Cathy when she spoke, and, at times, completed her sentences. When Cathy presented new ideas and suggestions to accomplish tasks using a different approach, her ideas were quickly dismissed by Amanda, with the explanation that Amanda's way of doing things was the best way. At one point, Cathy decided to keep her ideas and suggestions to herself, because she perceived that Amanda's viewpoint was a "need for control" and was convinced that she would not change. So, what started as an attempt to communicate transitioned into a fear of communication, as a result of constant negative feedback.

Where Are Your Questions?

As the weeks passed, Cathy's frustration grew even stronger. When a day passed, and she didn't ask Amanda any questions, Amanda would summon Cathy to her office, to inquire why. Cathy explained that she completely understood the work presented to her and didn't have any questions. Amanda responded with, "I don't trust somebody who doesn't ask questions." Cathy made numerous efforts to convince Amanda that if she had questions, she would address them to her, and that she had no reason not to trust her. Cathy wanted Amanda to understand that she was striving to work independently. Cathy felt as if she was talking to a brick wall, as Amanda restated her position that questions should be directed only to her, and emphasized that if questions were not being asked, then she had reason to be suspicious.

Cathy began to consider whether or not she should seek employment elsewhere. She grew weary, as she became paranoid that Amanda would always look over her shoulder and make her feel inadequate. Then she decided that this was a challenge that she must face and overcome and resolved that quitting would simply be an easy way out of the situation. She was also uncomfortable with the idea of starting all over again, at a new job, at the same time that she had planned to return to college. But her frustration escalated when one of her daily responsibilities, sorting the mail, was given to another employee to handle. Amanda felt that sorting the mail occupied too much of Cathy's time, and she wanted Cathy to use that time to reply to correspondence. Cathy found sorting the mail to be very beneficial because it afforded her the opportunity to familiarize herself with each account representative and the accounts they handled. Furthermore, much of the mail she sorted was handled by her, immediately, that day, rather than placing it in the account reps' in-boxes, where it might sit for two or three days before any action was taken on it. Eventually, the responsibility of mail sorting was given back to Cathy, as the other employee was misrouting too much correspondence.

Cathy's frustration at not being allowed to work independently deepened, and she wondered why Amanda treated her the way she did, and what she should do about it.

Shaking the Bird Cage (A)

by Teri C. Tompkins, University of Redlands

"I can't believe this! What do they think they are trying to pull?" Jim exploded.

Kathy shook her head, "I don't know—this just doesn't make sense."

Jim and Kathy sat in the lab where team members of the antenna team often gathered as they checked on their work projects. Three of the five senior staff members—Sylvia, Karen, and Kevin—were also present in the lab. They all stood around one of the lab tables, a look of concern on each of their faces.

Kathy had just seen an unofficial copy of an organization chart, which showed that the 17-member antenna team was being split. Three of the team members would maintain their connection with Dick, their current supervisor and world-renowned scientist for his knowledge about their product. The rest of the team would be assigned to Forrest—someone the team didn't know, and, from what they had heard, was a real "micromanager." He had a reputation for imposing his will on everyone he supervised. He didn't like to have his authority questioned. In addition, he was an administrator, not a real scientist. They felt sure he didn't know a thing about their product line.

Members of the Antenna Team

Members of the antenna team had worked long and hard to create a successful product line of sensor seeking devices. The 10 engineers were responsible for hardware and software design. The five technicians—noted for their exceptional skill—built prototypes and tested them. Dick, the team's manager and guru, was an eccentric sort. He was a genius when it came to knowledge about sensor equipment, but as a manager he lacked even the basic skill. To compensate for this problem, the team had a supervisor, Chuck. Chuck had a lot of project management and managerial experience, but he had very little knowledge or skill about sensor equipment. As a result, the highly technical team had little respect for him and saw him as a paper-pusher.

The two informal leaders of the Antenna team were Jim and Kathy. Jim was valued because he asked good questions, and challenged assumptions. Even though his personality tended toward seeing the negative in everything, the team found him extremely useful in improving their product line because he thought of questions they hadn't even considered. Kathy was the visionary of the group. She helped the team see possibilities. The team respected her engineering experience and valued her facilitative skills.

Change in the Air

The antenna team's projects were for the defense industry and came primarily from in-house subcontracts. In the past, the antenna team had been very successful at getting contracts for their work. However, with the shift of focus away from the defense industry, there was talk that the team would have to take more of their work to the commercial market. None of the members had any marketing experience and didn't know how to accomplish this. Chuck had told them that without success in the commercial market, their financial outlook did not look good; in fact, because of fewer defense contracts, their financial contribution to company profits had not been good for over a year.

Team Process

Members of the antenna team were a close-knit group. They often met around the copy machine or in the lab to chat about products, new projects, or even about personal matters. It hadn't always been that way. Kathy, who had been on the team for four years, was very instrumental in helping the team build cohesiveness and determine team goals. After Kathy came, the team began examining their work systems more systematically. There seemed to be less blaming for problems and more willingness to handle them. They consciously shared information and skills with each other and established clear goals. Members felt that they had a clear understanding of the skills that each of them possessed and that this helped them better coordinate their work requirements. As a result, projects were getting done closer to schedule or even ahead of schedule. In addition, the five early-career engineers seemed to be learning a lot from the midcareer engineers, like Kathy and Jim. Up until the recent financial crisis, the antenna team felt that they had been operating like a well-oiled machine.

Now they wondered what would happen to the team that they had worked so hard to build.

[Do not read Case B until instructed.]

Current Organization Chart

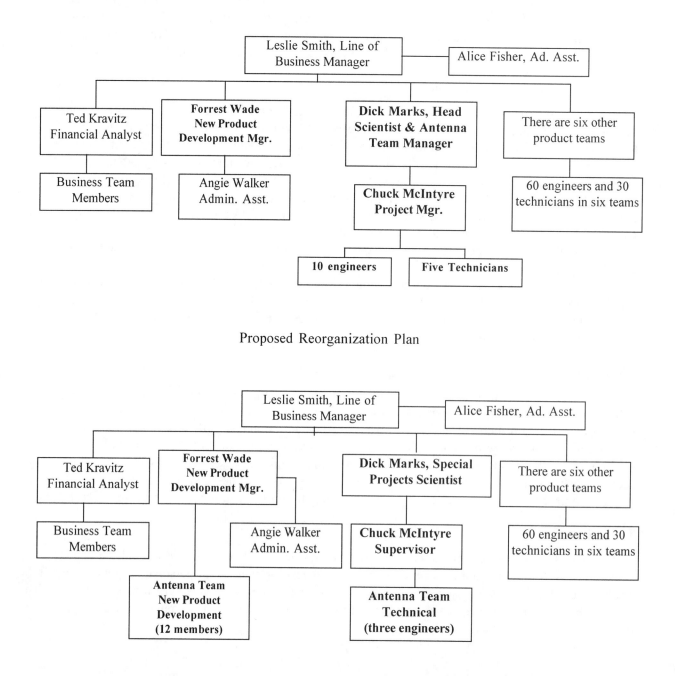

Proposed Reorganization Plan

Shaking the Bird Cage (B)

Kathy looked around the lab. Several more engineers had arrived and everyone looked upset. "Let's fight this," she said. "We've worked too hard to let them split us up like this."

"What can we do—quit en masse?" asked Karen.

"If we have to, yes!" Jim said.

"We know we are a good team," said Kathy, "but maybe they don't realize what a gem they have here. Let's tell them."

For the next hour, the team brainstormed about how important it was to keep them together. Kathy madly scribbled notes, as she and Jim led the discussion. Kathy summarized their concerns, which were primarily that the team worked efficiently together, had clear-cut goals, knew the strengths and weaknesses of their fellow team members, and needed to work closely together to get the synergy they had experienced over the past few years. They felt that breaking up the team would cost the company more in the long run because a new formation of the team would waste a lot of time (and money) before the new team learned to work together. In addition, they felt that they had plenty of skill and enthusiasm for the technical side, but they needed training on the managerial side to be more responsive to management's needs. They argued that they didn't need a new manager but a new staff person with marketing experience who could help the team take their products commercial. They didn't want to be managed but guided. They felt if they were given the resources, they would give 150 percent as they always had. "We have great team spirit—don't separate a great team," Kathy concluded.

Over the next several weeks, Kathy and Jim negotiated with top management about keeping their team together. Top management was surprised at the strong feelings the team had about the reorganization. They had been led to believe that the team didn't like Chuck or Dick and wouldn't mind the changes. In addition, top management had serious concerns about the lack of success that the team had been experiencing over the last 14 months. Team members argued that it was a result of economic changes. Forrest, the potential new manager, originator of the reorganization plan, argued that the team members were a bunch of egotists who didn't want anyone to manage them. He felt the team had lost its edge and cared more about each other than the good of the company. "Give me a few weeks with them, and I'll whip them into shape!" he told management.

Split Operations at Sky and Arrow Airlines

by Jeremy Offenstein

Jack had worked several jobs before, but his job at Sky Airlines was his all-time favorite. He actually enjoyed going to work. For one thing, it was fun; he and his coworkers would kid around a lot. On a nice, spring day, when it was slow, they would throw a Frisbee around on the ramp. It was not that this sort of activity was exactly approved of, but the company did have a casual attitude, and if the right supervisor was working, and all the work was done, it was not a problem. More important, the flights were sent out on time, with all passengers and all bags on board. Equally important, the customers were satisfied. This was work that Jack felt was easy, when a person enjoyed his job.

When Jack started to work for Sky, he was sent to Salt Lake City, Utah, for his company orientation and training. The importance of excellent customer service, to distinguish the airline from others, was emphasized. Other airlines flew the same routes for the same price and at about the same time; it was what the individual employee contributed to the customer's experience that distinguished Sky from the competition. At some point, the importance of safety at work was stressed. But what really caught Jack's attention was the emphasis placed on having fun at work. Anecdotes were told about the fun people had at Sky, including one story in which a ramper was tied up and loaded into the back of a plane (before sending it to its destination). Jack left the three-day orientation feeling like he worked for a company that recognized the individual employee as an important factor that determined the success of Sky. Jack perceived Sky as encouraging its employees to enjoy their job.

"Turning a Flight" at Sky

When Jack started work, he found that working out on the ramp, where the primary responsibilities were unloading bags and passengers off of flights, reloading them, and then sending the flights, was pretty exciting. All of these activities fell under the phrase "turning a flight." Sometimes he and his team had to act very quickly to turn a flight on time. This was particularly the case with flights headed for the Los Angeles International Airport (LAX). Flights going to LAX had to depart by a particular time given to them by LAX air traffic control. This was known as a flow time. When assigned a short flow time, it required a lot of teamwork, and the team had to move quickly. Jack grew to depend on the help of his team.

Jack recalled a time when five aircraft were down at the same time; two of these flights had tight flow times into LAX, while another two flights were already late, and the captains were screaming, on the radio, to operations to get their aircraft turned. "In the midst of chaos, we had a whole trailer of bags that needed to be loaded onto one of the LAX flights," Jack remembered. He continued, "On that particular trailer, there was a freight shipment that needed to connect with another flight at LAX. Therefore, the ramp crew decided that the plane with the box had to leave on time. The problem was the size of the box. It was too large for one person to lift it on board." Having five planes and three rampers, Jack and his coworkers were short on labor. Fortunately, the operations manager came out and loaded one of the flights. A ticket agent helped out as well, and the station manager came out and helped Jack load the bags and the freight onto the LAX flight with the box. Meanwhile, the captain had already fired up the engine, exposing Jack and his manager to a strong stream of hot exhaust. When all the planes were turned, Jack and his coworkers were proud to have worked together and to have met the demand.

Sky Culture

Camaraderie among Sky employees was reinforced by company functions. Some of these were informal parties arranged by individual employees. Others were formal parties put together by the company. One of these events was Sky's 25th anniversary party held in Los Angeles. At this party, they had good food, plenty to drink, and a music and slide show presentation demonstrating Sky employees enjoying their jobs while playing rock music.

In addition to the shared camaraderie and sense of synergy Jack felt with all Sky employees, he and the other rampers composed a "side team." These five individuals, Doug, Mike, Jim, Russ, and Frank, worked closely together with every flight. He and his five friends spent time outside of work together. They went to movies, bars, and parties in the college town next to the airport. The six of them often used their flight benefits to travel to places like Las Vegas. Jack, Doug, and Jim even went to Berlin and Amsterdam. Spending their time together, outside of work, helped build commitment among them. Because of this, Jack felt he could always count on one of them to help him out when in a bind at work.

Another benefit of the job was the flexibility of his schedule. Jack attended college, so at the beginning of every quarter he needed to change his work schedule to coincide with his class schedule. By collaborating with management and his coworkers, a conflict between school and work never occurred. Jack felt that he would not find such a great benefit at many jobs.

The airport was located at a southern California coastal city, Santa Clara, and the weather was often nearly perfect. Many days were spent working under sunny skies and temperatures in the low 70s. Even when the weather was bad, Jack enjoyed working outdoors. Though he knew it was somewhat absurd, Jack always felt pretty rugged, working in cold, windy, and rainy weather. He would stand there, feeling the cold rain running past his rain gear, down the collar of his shirt, panting from just loading 700 pounds of bags, and feeling proud to have handled it all so well.

The autonomy and empowerment that Jack was given at work also contributed to his satisfaction. The ramp was a large space, events could happen very quickly, and there was little direct supervision. Often Jack would have to make several decisions on his own and instruct his coworkers on what to do next. He enjoyed making decisions and felt that he was good at it. Jack took pride in knowing that, sometimes, he was individually responsible for getting a flight out on time. Another aspect of the autonomy that Jack liked was the extra time to interact with his coworkers when there was a lull in the number of flights. Unless something needed to be done, no one gave him work just to keep him busy.

Jack liked working at Sky and was bothered because he knew in six to eight months he would graduate from college, quit his job at Sky, and move to wherever he attended graduate school the following year. Little did Jack know that, soon, out of the blue, a dark cloud on the horizon would wipe away any remorse he had about quitting his job.

Merger with Arrow Airlines

Jack heard rumors about a plan for Sky to merge its operations with Arrow Airlines at Santa Clara Airport. During his time at Sky, Jack had observed that Arrow was much more formal than Sky. Arrow had procedures that were always followed. For example, Sky employees often commented on Arrow's use of belt loaders. When Arrow had a Boeing (737) on the ground, they would drive up their belt loaders shortly after the plane was parked. Because a 737 normally held between 100 to 200 bags, loading all of those bags by hand would have been exhausting. However, when an EMB (Brazilia), a much smaller plane, landed, Arrow would still use belt loaders. The Brazilia did not hold more than 60 bags, so using belt loaders took more time than just driving a cart up and unloading the bags by hand. The employees at Sky felt that using belt loaders on every flight was silly, since the policy had, obviously, been written with loading larger aircraft in mind. Nevertheless, this is how Arrow's employees did the job.

Arrow differed from Sky in other ways, as well. Arrow, a large, world-class carrier, was much better known than Sky. Jack attributed this factor to the arrogance he felt was portrayed by Arrow's employees. When the rumor of the merger became a reality, and the two airlines merged their operations at Santa Clara, Jack became more familiar with Arrow employees' perceptions.

Jack wondered if their difference in age or company size explained why each group of employees harbored different viewpoints of their jobs. The employees at Arrow were older than the Sky employees and referred to themselves as "professional rampers." Jack and his fellow rampers went into hysterics.

They perceived "professional" as carrying out their duties with a stern face. They worked at Sky for other reasons, such as the flight benefits or an interest in becoming a pilot.

Split Operations

As part of the merger, Arrow management decided that operations would be split between the two companies. Arrow employees would ticket, check in, and board all passengers. Sky employees would handle all of the ramp work, such as bag loading and unloading, deboarding the plane, and giving Arrow's gate the go-ahead to begin boarding, parking, and sending the aircraft.

When the split operations began, everyone on the ramp at Sky felt like a fish out of water. Before the transition, Sky ran about 30 flights per day for Delta Airlines. After the transition, Sky ran about 30 flights per day for Arrow and about seven flights per day for Delta. The Delta flights would continue to be run exclusively by Sky employees. The basic structure was easy enough to understand, but Jack soon noticed that the details became complicated.

Procedures, in many cases, were unclear and conflict escalated. Jack recalled an event that occurred the Wednesday before Thanksgiving. The airport was packed, delays and cancellations were on the rise, due to the weather, and flights arriving or departing at Santa Clara, ranging from San Francisco to San Diego, were held back. To make matters worse, conflict arose between Arrow and Sky regarding which flights were a priority.

There were four flights, delayed by the air traffic control at LAX, on the ground en route to LAX. Arrow Ops called the Sky employees and told them that one of their airplanes had called in and authorized a LAX departure, if Sky could have its wheels up in 20 minutes. To make this happen, they would have to load the aircraft with as many bags as possible and get it boarded, with the thirty passengers, within 15 minutes. Jack called Arrow's gate and asked them to begin boarding. At that time, Arrow's gate was already boarding its San Francisco flight. Arrow showed no interest in initiating the boarding of the LAX flight, although in the past they had successfully boarded both flights simultaneously. Jack asked Arrow, once again, to begin boarding the LAX flight.

Meanwhile, Mike and Doug, in the midst of rain and slippery surfaces, were frantically trying to load as many bags as possible onto the flight. With less than 10 minutes to have the wheels up, Jack, frustrated from Arrow's lack of urgency, marched over to Arrow's gate and pleaded with them to begin boarding the passengers. After being ignored by Arrow's employees, Jack, feeling useless, sulked back to the LAX flight and explained the situation to the captain. Despite his explanation, the captain was very upset that they missed their release time and were delayed another half-hour.

Job responsibility became the epicenter of conflict between the employees of the two companies. For example, when late-checked bags were processed and placed on the belt by Arrow, they accepted no responsibility of notifying Sky that additional bags needed to be loaded on the aircraft. Arrow's employees maintained this perception regarding flight releases. Although the flight releases were printed in Arrow's stations, they accepted no responsibility of bringing them out to the aircraft, if there was no Sky employee available to pick them up. Jack felt that, at times, there was no cooperation between the two companies.

Disputes often arose over which company was responsible for performance failures. In a meeting, Sky's station manager advised Jack and the other rampers that Arrow's station management had complained about the failures of Sky's operations for Arrow. Specific complaints were that bags missed their flights, aircraft were sent too early, and aircraft were delayed. Jack and the other rampers felt that Arrow had fixed the blame, for these incidents, on Sky's employees. Jack and the other rampers left the meeting feeling angry and unsupported by either of the two companies. The rampers began to refer to all of Arrow's employees as stupid and incompetent. Arrow's complaints about Sky's employees continued, as Sky's employees began to complain regularly to their supervisors and station manager about Arrow's employees. Still, Sky's employees felt that their issues never went beyond their managers' ears.

More Rumors

Approximately three months into the split operations, rumors of Arrow taking over all ground operations began to surface. If Arrow took over, Sky would now service seven flights, instead of 37 flights. Talk of layoffs began to travel among Sky employees. Jack, looking for facts, and questioning rumors, waited to see what would happen next.

Jack hoped that some more Delta flights would be added to Sky's schedule. He also considered the possibility that Arrow would not take over the ground operations at all. Jack wondered if Arrow was prepared to hire several more employees and increase their operating expense. If he were lucky, Arrow would take over after Jack left the airport, since he would only work there for another six to nine months.

Over the next few weeks, speculations and opinions about what would happen escalated among Sky employees. Some thought that nearly everyone would lose their jobs, while others thought that few or none would lose their jobs. When Jack and other employees frequently asked management about what was going to happen, they did not get any answers. Although management denied any knowledge of what was happening, Jack suspected that they were not being truthful with him.

A month had gone by since the layoff rumors began. Jack was closing up the second to the last aircraft for the night and decided to get some rest until the last flight was ready. He headed into the Sky station, looking for Doug, who was working with him that night. Jack found Doug with another coworker, Andrew, and his supervisor, Elizabeth, talking about what was going to happen with the Arrow and Sky operations. Elizabeth told them that Arrow would take over the entire ground operation in the near future. She explained that about one-third of Sky's employees would definitely be laid off. Jack suddenly realized that based on his seniority, he was almost out of a job.

After only a few months into the split operations, upper management decided to scrap the plan and lay everyone off. Jack felt cheated and very angry. Because management failed to put any effort into making the split operations work, the employees would be punished for their failure, and lose their jobs. He also considered that this would mess up his ability to continue to pay rent on his apartment until the lease ran out. Then Jack focused on what Andrew was saying. He realized that Andrew had been talking about how he was going to use his flight benefits that summer. Jack yelled at him, "What are you talking about? You're not even going to have a damn job!"

Temporary Employees: Car Show Turned Ugly (A)

by Gary Oddou, Utah State University

For the third time, Temporary Employment Agency (TEA) had been hired by Research Corporation (RC) to staff the car show in San Jose, California. A major auto manufacturer needed some research done to decide which sport car design elements buyers wanted in this type of car.

TEA had hired its temporary staff for the show and Joan Walters, the supervisor for TEA, thought everything was going as scheduled until the orientation meeting the day before the show. The temporary employees were asking for two extra days pay they felt they were due. Sue, the apparent leader of the complaining temporary employees, spoke forcefully: "TEA obligated us to commit to the entire 5 days during the interviews or said we wouldn't be hired." As a result, many of the temporaries were counting on that income and had made arrangements to work the five days.

Joan, TEA's supervisor for the show, denied that TEA had obligated the employees to work the entire schedule and was not willing to okay payment for the extra two days. As the tension mounted, the 18 temporary employees threatened to walk off the job, effectively shutting the car show down. If they walked, in one day TEA would have to interview, hire and orient a new set of temporaries. Although it could be done using all its resources, it was not an enviable option, either. Joan stood there in front of the resentful audience, feeling like the heat had just been turned up. Time was running out.

TEA—Some Background

Temporary Employment Agency (TEA), a local, well-known temporary manpower agency in Santa Clara, had been in business about 15 years. It had been recently bought by a national firm located in Texas and there was some sentiment that it was under pressure to be a good profit center. It was a temporary employment agency, recruiting temporary employees for a variety of jobs, but mostly specializing in the high-technology industry. It employed over 25 staff members. It brought in several million dollars of revenues and appeared to be very successful in placing its applicants. Management had considerable experience in the temporary employment business and represented a diverse group in terms of gender and ethnic background.

The Market Research Firm: RC

On this occasion, Research Corporation had contracted with TEA to hire 18 temporary employees to staff the car show. Research Corporation (RC) was a well-established market research firm from Chicago. Ford Motor Company had retained them to determine buyer preferences in sports cars. Research subjects were selected based on demographic profiles that fit the auto manufacturer's typical sport car buyers. The source of information about these buyers came from surveys they filled out as recent sport car purchasers from this same auto manufacturer. Subjects were each paid $100 for their participation. Each participant wore a monitor strapped on in front and gave feedback as questions were asked about each car to determine the most desirable features. There were five cars. The complete tour took about an hour.

The Temporary Employees: Their Recruitment and the Interview

Shelley Shurman, a TEA employee, had contacted a friend who was a member of a local church and who had a network of friends in that same church. Shelley thought this would be a quick and easy way to get responsible individuals to help staff the show. She asked if her friend would contact the necessary person in the local parish to announce that a job opportunity was available for a number of people who were interested in working a "car show" for a few days. Shelley's friend immediately contacted the head of the women's suborganization in their parish to start the networking process. There were a number of women in this organization who did not work outside the home and so this would be an ideal opportunity to earn some extra money without a long-term job commitment.

In fact, many of these temporary employees were housewives and took the job expressly to earn money for Christmas. Some had already arranged and committed to day care for the weekdays they would be working; a few others already had jobs but took days off to work the show because it paid better.

One woman, a former member of the local parish referred to earlier, even flew in from Portland, Oregon. Based on her understanding of the five-day commitment and intended income, the pay she would receive for doing the show for five days would cover her plane ticket. Since she was from the San Jose area originally, she saw it as an opportunity to see friends and family as well. Because of recent long-term unemployment in the family, she otherwise would not have had the money to justify such a trip.

Nine of the 18 women and men were members of the church and most had known one another for years, meeting together every Sunday and having other outside-of-church responsibilities that required monthly interaction and often a great deal of phone contact to organize activities and such. One young man, also a member of the same church, had just graduated from high school and was working a lower-paying job. He saw this as a way to earn some extra money to help pay for his education. Another was a college student who had a flexible work schedule and was getting married, so he was motivated to earn some extra money also.

Each potential hire was asked to come down to TEA to be interviewed, decide which job she was interested in and sign a contract. At the interview, each person filled out an application and then went through a very brief interview. The interviewer quickly looked over the application and then began to explain the various jobs available at the show and showed each potential hire the sheet with the various jobs (see Exhibit A). Each interviewee selected a job and was then asked to come back the next day, the same day as the orientation that evening, to sign a W-2 form and to sign the agreement they had been given orally during the interview (see Exhibit B).

The Contract Dispute

On June 5th, the women and the others went to the scheduled orientation the day before the auto show. Many of them carpooled since they were used to organizing themselves and had become good friends from their years of association. To their surprise, at the orientation, they were told their work would only cover two days (plus the half day orientation). This meant that they would get two days less pay than they had been anticipating. Since many of the women had made day care arrangements and were counting on this money for Christmas gifts and such and others for educational expenses, they were clearly not happy at this disappointing news.

At the orientation, each employee was again given a specific listing of the different jobs to be done but this time with the dates and times associated with the job (See Exhibit C). With the exception of one or two job categories, all other jobs were listed to work June 6 through June 8 instead of the full length of the show dates from the June 6 to June 10 (which is what the temporary help was allegedly told even though some of the exhibit material actually shows June 6–11 on the masthead). Joan Walters, the TEA supervisor, explained that the work schedule covered the half-day orientation and the two days of conducting the actual research (June 6–8).

At this point, a major problem developed. A number of the temporary employees said that the during their interview at TEA, the interviewer emphasized that all employees had to work the entire project from June 6 through June 10 and possibly into June 11. The temporary employees said they had to sign an agreement to work "the entire project" (Exhibit B) and were told they couldn't be hired if they could not commit to the entire time. (Three employees, including the two young men mentioned earlier, were, in fact, required to work the entire schedule and so they had no quarrel with TEA. Their jobs included running errands and setting up and taking down the show.)

One temporary employee said that at the interview she had been shown last year's contract and that, indeed, the part of the show that involved most of the temporary employees was only two and one-half days. When she asked her TEA interviewer about that, she (allegedly like the others) had been told the show would require a five-day commitment, the interviewer supposedly told her that the contract she (the interviewee) had seen was from a previous show and did not reflect the present car show.

The actual signed agreement (Exhibit B) did not state the dates of the show. That information was allegedly communicated orally by the interviewers until the following day when at the orientation, the temporary help saw the sheet with the actual dates and times they would be working (see Exhibit C).

Although the monetary loss from two days less pay did not represent a large sum (close to $200 gross per employee), the temporary employees felt that TEA had misrepresented the situation. On principle, if not legally, they felt TEA should pay them for the entire time to which they were allegedly made to commit to.

Still further complicating the situation for TEA, when this whole issue came to a head at the orientation meeting, the day before the show, a Research Corporation representative (the individual representing the firm subcontracting to TEA for the staffing of the auto show) sided with the temporary employees. Whether he was aware of the alleged oral commitment during the interview or not, or aware of previous car show contracts, was not clear.

Shelley, the TEA employee originally responsible for the recruitment of the temporary employees that were part of the same parish, was apparently embarrassed by the demands of these church members. Shelley took the side of TEA and some bad feelings developed between her and some of the others recruited through her networking.

Other allegations were made on both sides, implying collusion and dishonesty. Because approximately half of the temporary employees asking for complete payment were members of the same church, Sue, the most outspoken temporary employee, and some of the other women, felt TEA suspected them of colluding on the matter beforehand in an attempt to get more money. The temporary help thought that to save face, the interviewers probably got together and lied about what they had told those interviewing. And if they didn't, then management was to blame. In either case, the temporary help felt TEA should take responsibility and TEA felt the new hires were exaggerating an issue in an unfair way just to get more money.

In addition, the day of the show itself, Shelley had allegedly been told by TEA staff that some of the temporaries had been swearing at TEA employees and were generally uncooperative. Apparently believing the reports, Shelley reported to her original contact and friend in the parish from which the women were recruited that their behavior was totally inappropriate

In fact, the association between the "demanding employees" and their church membership became a very visible issue. The feelings were intense enough that the local church leader of these members (a highly respected manufacturing engineer in Silicon Valley start-up circles) was asked to come down and talk to TEA management and the women at the show. He did so, talking to several of the women in his parish and to Shelley. After talking to both sides, he came to the conclusion that the TEA employees, though perhaps not intentionally, were probably at fault and the allegations of swearing and uncooperative behavior were imagined. He did not become formally involved to mediate the demands as he felt that was inappropriate. He also determined for himself that the allegations of swearing and uncooperative behavior were simply that—allegations.

In the future, the local church leader made it clear to the head of the women's organization in the parish that no such requests for employment or other such activity from the "outside" were to be formally handled by any part of the church organization.

Leadership among the Temporary Employees

Throughout the whole process of trying to resolve the dispute, the temporary employees enjoyed the strong leadership of Sue McIntyre. She had been a real estate agent for the last several years and presented herself with great self-confidence. She and her husband had three children and, like many of the others, she was looking forward to some extra Christmas money.

Sue was the most vocal at the orientation. She spontaneously verbalized the issue and garnered support from a number of other temporary employees. Although not all the temporary employees spoke up, one women's opinion was particularly helpful in soldifying Sue's position. Jeanne Faure, the president of the women's organization in their church, agreed that there had been misrepresentation in her interview and also felt that TEA had a moral obligation to pay them for the entire show. All of the temporary help signed a letter that Sue had written to TEA requesting the additional payment for the two days (See Exhibit E).

In TEA's defense, one of TEA's management team said that in the signed agreement, it mentions specifically that "The hours scheduled are what is expected, but there are many variables involved." (Refer to Exhibit B) Therefore, even if TEA interviewers had told them they must be available to work for 5 days, there was no legal obligation on the part of TEA to do so.

Sue and the others didn't recall that passage and felt that even though it was there, TEA misrepresented the situation by insisting orally that the temporary help must be available the entire five days. She and others felt that since this was at least the third time the show had occurred, past experience should have dictated clearly how much time TEA would need the temporary help so they shouldn't be told one thing and then another.

In addition to Sue's clear stance and leadership, a male member of the group but not a member of the same church, also complained that there had been misrepresentation. His position was that TEA was clearly in the wrong. Based on his understanding of the laws (he had just finished law school and was awaiting the results of the bar exam), he felt legal action could be taken if necessary and made that known to TEA during the orientation in front of all the employees.

The Hour of Reckoning

A vice president of TEA, Anita Johnson, was summoned to the meeting from her home after a quick briefing of the situation by Joan, TEA's car show supervisor. As Anita stepped up to the podium to address the employees' demand, she clearly felt the tenseness in the atmosphere and the anticipation of the temporary employees.

[Please do not read Case B until instructed to do so.]

Temporary Employment: Car Show Turned Ugly (B)

Having been briefed about the situation before arriving, Anita took time to mull over the situation as she was driving to the meeting. She decided to pay the two days equivalent pay although she did not admit any guilt on TEA's part to the temporary help. In subsequent correspondence to each employee (Exhibit D), TEA called this money "a gift," stating that it did not feel obligated legally to pay this money and could, later on, decide to recover this money by legal means.

A week later, Anita wrote another letter (see Exhibit E) to all temporary employees saying that a number of temporaries had contacted TEA to say that they did not share the other temporaries' opinion and had felt coerced into signing the "demands letter" with the other employees. Others, TEA said in the letter, notified them to say they had been solicited to sign the "demand letter" but did not agree with the demands.

Sue, the informal leader, quickly contacted all the others to explain that she thought TEA was attempting to weaken their stand by making these claims. Sue discovered that the letter had indeed weakened a few temporaries' resolve to pursue the extra two days' payment due to the "legal-sounding language," as one temporary reportedly put it.

John Sorden, the law student among the temporary employees, volunteered to represent the group if a suit were necessary.

In this same letter, TEA required each temporary who wanted the extra pay to sign and date the letter (Exhibit E) to reattest each person's interest in receiving the extra payment. Fourteen employees did so and did receive the extra payment.

Exhibit A

EXTERIOR CLINIC, PHOEINX, ARIZONA
June 6-11, 1999
TEMPORARY AGENCY POSITIONS

SUPERVISOR:

Responsible for <u>managing</u> agency personnel, including scheduling of breaks, lunches, and tracking daily the number of hours worked for each employee. Also responsible to make sure all agency persons show up and are on time. This individual will be stationed at Check-In.

CHECK-IN ATTENDANT:

Greet respondent. Verity demographic information and vehicle ownership, prepare questionnaire with respondent number and additional information, and direct respondent to next survey room.

CHECK-OUT ATTENDANT:

Responsible for paying respondents incentive and recruiting them for focus groups.

"STAND-BY" ATTENDANT (GOPHER):

Run errands and miscellaneous tasks. Requires the use of his/her personal vehicle, mileage reimbursed. <u>Must</u> be familiar with local and surrounding areas.

RELIEF:

Will be trained for all positions in order to fill in for those taking breaks and lunches.

STRAPPERS:

Responsible for securing computer comfortably to respondent. Will instruct respondent to proceed to the Pre-Clinic/Video Room.

TABLE ATTENDANT (Pre-Clinic/Video):

Great respondent. Instruct them to watch the video. Answer any questions they may have. Make sure respondents arc comfortable working with the computer. Direct, respondent to next survey room.

SKETCH ROOM STARTER:

Greet respondent. Responsible for looking over the questionnaire and "starting" the respondent on the next portion of the questionnaire.

INTERIOR ROOM STARTER:

Greet respondent. Responsible for looking over the questionnaire and "starting" the respondent on the next portion of the questionnaire.

STYLE ROOM ATTENDANT:

Great respondent. Responsible for handing out the next portion of the questionnaire, reviewing the questionnaire for completeness and directing the respondents to the next portion of the survey.

WHEEL EVALUATION ATTENDANT:

Greet respondent, Responsible for walking the respondent through the wheel evaluation section of the clinic.

CONSOLE:

Greet respondent. Responsible for walking respondents though this portion of the clinic. Making sure that the respondent understands what he or she is to evaluate.

EXTERIOR EVALUATION:

Greet respondent. Responsible for looking over the questionnaire and "starting" the respondent in the correct area, also answering any questions that may pertain to this portion of the clinic.

FLOATER:

Greet respondent. Responsible for directing respondent to different sections of the clinic.

Exhibit B

TEMPORARY EMPLOYMENT AGENCY
A division of ATR International
═══

2401 Alameda Dr.
Tempe, AZ 85282-1137
FAX: 602-967-1171
TEL: 602-494-1214

Dear Temporary Employment Employee:

We are pleased you will be working the Research Corporation. Please review the following <u>very important</u> <u>information:</u>

CUSTOMER:	Research Corporation
LOCATION:	Phoenix Civic Auditorium
	Hall A/B
	Park Avenue and Cactus Street
	Phoenix, AZ 85282

DIRECTIONS:	See attached directions
DUTIES:	See Attachment I
SCHEDULE:	See Attachment II

TIME SHEETS: Please follow the instructions attached in completing your time sheets. Additional time sheets are available from the project supervisor.

HOURLY RATE: $9.00 per hour. Lunch breaks are not paid. Overtime is paid per Arizona state regulations.

LUNCH-BREAKS: Please take a sack lunch for your convenience. There will be a refrigerator on the premises for employees. Lunch breaks are 30 minutes unless instructed otherwise.

Temporary Employment Agency and RC requires that **<u>everyone work the entire project!</u>** There is a lengthy training session involved and we **<u>cannot</u>** replace you once the project has begun. If you believe that something may occur to prevent you from committing to, and completing the entire project, we must be notified immediately. The hours scheduled are what is expected, but there are many variables involved. Therefore, we ask that you please be flexible to accommodate the needs of RC.

Thank you all. I know you will enjoy the project! Please call us at (602) 623-1520 if you have any questions.

Sincerely,

Temporary Employment Agency

I have read and received a copy of
these instructions and agree to meet
all commitments described above.
X_____

Exhibit C

EXTERIOR CLINIC-PHOENIX, ARIZONA
June 6-11, 1999
TEMPORARY AGENCY REQUIREMENTS / SCHEDULE

POSITION	NUMBER		DATES	TIMES
Supervisor	1	Training	6/6	2:30 p.m. - 6:30 p.m.
		Operation	6/7	7:30 a.m. - 10:00 p.m.
			6/8	7:30 a.m. - 10:00 p.m.
Check-In	2	Training	6/6	3:00 a.m. - 6:00 p.m.
		Operation	6/7	7:30 a.m. - 8:00 p.m.
			6/8	7:30 a.m. - 8:00 p.m.
	1	Focus Groups	6/9	3:30 p.m. - 8:30 p.m.
	1	Focus Groups	6/10	3:30 p.m. - 8:30 p.m.
Check-Out	2	Training	6/6	3:00 p.m. - 6:00 p.m.
		Operation	6/7	9:00 a.m. - 10:00 p.m.
			6/8	9:00 a.m. - 10:00 p.m.
"Stand-By" Attendant (Gopher)	1	Set-up	6/6	8:30 a.m. - 10:00 p.m.
		Operation	6/7	8:00 a.m. - 10:00 p.m.
			6/8	8:00 a.m. - 10:00 p.m.
			6/9	8:00 a.m. - 10:00 p.m.
			6/10	8:00 a.m. - 10:00 p.m.
Relief	2	Training	6/6	3:00 p.m. - 6:00 p.m.
		Operation	6/7	9:00 a.m. - 9:00 p.m.
			6/8	9:00 a.m. - 9:00 p.m.
Strappers	3	Training	6/6	3:00 p.m. - 6:00 p.m.
		Operation	6/7	7:30 a.m. - 8:00 p.m.
			6/9	7:30 a.m. - 8:00 p.m.
Pre-Clinic	1	Training	6/6	3:00 p.m. - 6:00 p.m.
		Operation	6/7	7:30 a.m. - 8:30 p.m.
			6/8	7:30 a.m. - 8:30 p.m.
Sketch Room Starter	1	Training	6/6	3:00 p.m. - 6:00 p.m.
		Operation	6/7	8:30 a.m. - 10:00 p.m.
			6/9	8:30 a.m. - 10:00 p.m.
Interior Room Starter	1	Training	6/6	3:00 p.m. - 6:00 p.m.
		Operation	6/7	8:30 a.m. - 10:00 p.m.
			6/8	8:30 a.m. - 10:00 p.m.
Style	1	Training	6/6	3:00 p.m. - 6:00 p.m.
		Operation	6/7	9:00 a.m. - 10:00 p.m.
			6/8	9:00 a.m. - 10:00 p.m.
Wheel Evaluation	2	Training	6/6	3:00 p.m. - 6:00 p.m.
		Operation	6/7	8:30 a.m. - 10:00 p.m.
			6/8	8:30 a.m. - 10:00 p.m.

Exhibit D

TEMPORARY EMPLOYMENT AGENCY
A division of ATR International

2401 Alameda Dr.
Tempe, AZ 85282-1137
FAX: 602-967-1171
TEL: 602-494-1214

June 7, 1999

Dear Employee:

You have demanded additional pay for the RC job we originally hired you to staff. You have threatened to strike and walk off the job if you do not receive this pay.

We agree to pay you the additional pay as a gift. We do so to protect our customer.

Temporary Employment Agency does not believe this payment or this letter creates a legal or contractual obligation to pay you beyond the terms of the original schedule.

We would like to see the RC job completed successfully. Please focus on the job at hand. If you have any questions, please contact Joan Walters, V.P., Temporary Employment Agency at 602-623-1782.

Jodi Harris, Payroll Manager

Exhibit E

TEMPORARY EMPLOYMENT AGENCY
A division of ATR International

===

2401 Alameda Dr.
Tempe, AZ 85282-1137
FAX: 602-967-1171
TEL: 602-494-1214

June 15, 1999

Dear Employee:

We have been contacted by some employees who have volunteered that they were not in agreement with the demands in the attached letter. Even though they felt influenced to sign it, they no longer wish to pursue the matter. Further, we have been notified by other employees on the assignment that they were solicited to sign the letter but refused to do so because they were in disagreement with the demands.

As you might remember, during your employment at the RC project, Temporary Employment Agency was threatened with an unauthorized work stoppage by employees in an effort to renegotiate terms of employment. Our concern for our client compelled us to award a one-time gift to <u>certain</u> employees, in return for an agreement not to strike. In view of the timing and duress under which we agreed to the gift, we would like to verify that you indeed signed the attached letter and that you intend to pursue your demand for those funds.

Your signature appears on the attached letter, pursuant to your assignment on the RC project for the period of 6/6/99 to 6/8/99. We would like to verify the following: 1) that the signature on the letter is actually yours; 2) that you continue to seek the gift specified in the attached letter.

Please check the appropriate box as shown below. Your signed return of this document by 6/24/99 will be our authorization to proceed. If you have any questions regarding these issues, please feel free to call me at 602-967-1171.

I wish to pursue the "gift" as pursuant to the attached letter No_____ Yes_____

Signed_____

Dated_____

Respectfully,

Jodi Harris
Payroll Manager

The Day They Announced the Buyout

by Diane Traschel

As Diane Fox walked up the stairs to work on June 15, 1997, it was just like any other day. When she reached the top of the stairs, she saw a sea of faces, full of shock and confusion. She thought to herself, "What are these people doing here?" She then remembered there was a training class that day. But why were they all standing around with a look of bewilderment on their faces? Why weren't they in the training class, learning the new Operations procedures?

A coworker ran up to her and said, "Did you hear the news?" She then realized that she was now one of those faces full of shock and confusion. Another bank had made an offer to buy their bank!

History of Rolling Hills Bank

Rolling Hills Bank was a small independent bank, located in the Orange County area of southern California. The bank was opened in 1982. It started out with a group of investors and one branch in the Placentia area. It slowly grew into a bank with six branches and 150 employees located throughout Orange County. Most of the branches were smaller independent banks that Rolling Hills had purchased or acquired during a Federal Deposit Insurance Corporation (FDIC) shutdown. The main groups of investors still owned their stock and were members of the board of directors. They were all friends who owned their own businesses, and were Board members during their free time. They often went out together on weekends, played golf, and spent the holidays at one another's houses. In 1997, the Board members mentioned during a meeting that they needed more free time. They even joked to the president, "When are we going to sell this place?"

At one time, in 1995, the bank was under a cease and desist order; the bank had made some imprudent loans. As a result of the order, a regulatory agency associated with the FDIC had to approve any loans that the bank wanted to make. The order was eventually lifted and the bank became very profitable. It was ranked as one of the highest independent banks in the *Orange County Register* two years in a row. The members of the board of directors were ready to enjoy their retirement instead of attending meetings and worrying over the profitability of the bank. When an offer was made, they couldn't turn it down.

Process of Growth at Rolling Hills Bank

When Rolling Hills bought a bank, it went through a process of assimilation. It retained most of the line, or branch, personnel and few, if any, corporate administrative personnel. Generally speaking, when a bank was for sale, it went to the highest bidder. If there was a bank that was not performing well, strategic investors and business developers would decide if the bank was worth buying. If so, an offer was made to that bank. The bank then decided whether to accept the offer. Once a bid was accepted, the buyout process would be completed in about four to six months.

When acquiring a bank because of an FDIC shutdown, several banks make bids, secretly, to the FDIC. The FDIC decided through due-diligence procedures which bank was allowed to purchase the remaining loans and accounts of a bank, once it was shut down. Customers did not know when their bank was going to be shut down, so their accounts were still open in the bank. When a bank was bought, an announcement was made, usually in the newspaper, and customers had the opportunity to close their accounts and take their business elsewhere.

California State Bank

The bank that had made the offer to buy Rolling Hills was California State Bank, a bank run by two brothers, with its corporate headquarters in West Covina, California. It had 14 branch locations in the Orange County, Pomona, and Riverside area of southern California, with around 250 employees, one fourth of them located in their corporate headquarters. This number was average for banks that had their own service center and data processing departments. However, Cal State Bank did not have an internal service center or data processing department, which made its headcount high. It had grown in the same fashion as Rolling Hills Bank with a series of purchases and acquisitions, but at a faster rate. With one more acquisition or purchase, it could become a billion dollar bank.

Situation

Diane began as a temporary employee during a Christmas break from college. Her Dad was the controller for the bank, and he told her they needed some administrative help. She was called in to help answer phones and to wrap 1,500 sets of coasters that were to be given to current shareholders as a gift. From there she became a clerk, assisting various departments, but reporting to the president's secretary. She kept her ears open and asked lots of questions. She learned fast and realized part-time clerical help was not what she wanted to do. A secretarial position opened up in the human resources department. She had assisted them before in various projects, and they were interested in hiring her. She decided to accept the position and continue her education at night.

She continued to learn more about the company and more about her position. She received confidential information from her supervisor and from her dad who helped her understand things that were happening, or going to happen. She was never shocked by anything that happened because she was usually forewarned. The crucial day that she walked into work was the first day she was unprepared for something involving the company.

The Offer

When Diane walked up the stairs that morning, she could instantly sense that something was wrong. A coworker ran up to her and said, "Did you hear what happened?" It was hard to believe that the words she heard next might lead to ending her employment at the bank. When she told her "No," her coworker informed Diane that this morning's paper stated that California State Bank had made an offer to buy Rolling Hills Bank. Rolling Hills Bank was considering the offer. Diane was shocked. "How could this happen?" she thought. "We just bought a bank, so why would someone offer to buy us? How could someone afford to buy us?"

All of these thoughts were running through her head, when her coworker said, "I can't believe they didn't tell us. Don't you think they should have warned us? Do you think we are going to lose our jobs?" Diane agreed with her; then the fear and confusion set in.

She now looked like the rest of the employees who were standing around. They were all talking about the same thing, "What's going to happen now?" She started thinking about what would happen if she lost her job. She could find another one, she thought. But then she realized her dad would lose his job, too. She still lived at home so she really began to worry. As she was listening to how the news got passed along from the newspaper, to a branch manager, who called her coworker and another manager and so on and so on, the president walked in, and said he would like to talk to everyone. The president had been one of the original investors in the bank, and had served as president for the bank's 15-year history. He was the type of person who needed his employees to like him and think highly of him. To strengthen this image, he said he would always let the employees know what was going on with the organization. Because of his promises, this situation caused some employees to distrust him now.

When the president began to speak, Diane was still thinking about possible solutions and outcomes of what would happen. The president explained the following:

- Though a very good offer had been made, a lot of due diligence must be done before anything was final. There was a possibility that the offer would fall through or be declined.
- Employees were not to panic; no one was losing their job, as of right now.
- He apologized for not telling them before the media got hold of the information.
- He also mentioned that he was not going to be a part of the new organization, if there was one, so he could not guarantee anyone their jobs.

The entire time he was speaking, he was fidgeting from foot to foot, putting his hands in and out of his pockets, and looking sorrowful about the news. How could he be sad if nothing was definite? Did he feel badly about the situation? He then offered to answer questions. For the next 20 minutes he reassured individuals that this was not supposed to be a secret, and that he meant to tell everyone himself. Since he said he would always be honest with them, some of the employees believed him, but others did not. After he finished, everyone appeared to be numb. He really had not told them anything they didn't already know. They all wanted reassurance that they weren't going to lose their jobs, and they didn't get it.

After the president left, the employees tried to get on with their day. It was difficult. When Diane's supervisor arrived, she asked her if she knew beforehand. She told Diane the president had called her at home the night before and let her know. She gave Diane more details. None of them reassured her. For instance, they wanted to keep all of the branches open and retain the individuals who worked there. They wanted to keep the service center and data processing department because they did not have one. But most likely, much of the administrative staff would not be needed.

Diane asked her, "Do you really think Rolling Hills will accept the offer?"

She told her, "The offer is bigger than any other one they have ever received. Plus, the shareholders have not received much in dividends and returns from their stock. They will most likely support the sale because they will receive the biggest gain from doing so, especially the president, since he has been here from the beginning."

At that point, Diane's fear and confusion turned to anger. How could one person be so greedy? How could ten people be so greedy to put 30 to 60 individuals out of work? Didn't they have any compassion? Did they ever think of anyone but themselves? Her anger died quickly, but her resentment did not. She went back to work.

By lunchtime, the buzz about the sale was raging. The training participants were taking a break, and they wanted to be filled in on anything they might have missed by being in the class. Diane did her best to reassure them the way she was instructed. But all the while, she was feeling like she had been betrayed. The employees of Rolling Hills Bank had been sold out. She decided to go talk to her dad and see what he thought. Her dad had been in the banking business since he graduated from college. In that time he had experienced numerous mergers and acquisitions. Since he had experience in this area, she thought he could give her some necessary advice and information.

Her dad was located in another building but at the same location. She walked over, and by the sound of things, it almost appeared that the place was empty. It usually was pretty quiet in the executive area but this was eerie. She went to her dad's office and sat down. When she sat down, she knew what he was thinking. The ever conservative banker told her, "It is too early to tell, and too early to get worked up about it. There are too many things that can change or go wrong. They don't have the only say in this. If we don't like the deal we can say, 'No.'" She knew he believed this because of his past experience in buyout situations. It made her feel a little better. She then asked him if he thought the president would fight to make the employees part of the deal. The president had mentioned earlier that "I plan on doing whatever I can to help you keep your jobs. Unfortunately, I am not going to be retained by the bank, so I cannot guarantee anything." Her Dad said he didn't know for sure. However, individuals at Cal State Bank already performed most of the administrative functions. She asked him if he was going to start looking for another job. He told her, "It is way too early to start doing that." Hearing that made her feel better. If a family man wasn't worried about losing his job, then she didn't need to be either.

She went back to her department and told anyone who asked her what she thought, or what she was going to do—that it was too early to tell. Part of her was still struggling with the feeling of uncertainty. Hearing others worry about their jobs and future influenced her fears. She had already had so many changes in her life that she was not ready for another one. Everyone told her that she didn't need to worry because she was "young and cheap" compared to other employees. If the new bank didn't hire her, she could easily find another job. She didn't know how true that was, but it did make her feel a little better. As expected, productivity was very low that day. By 2:00 P.M., employees were sitting around talking about the "what ifs" again. Diane's supervisor decided to have a department meeting.

Her department consisted of four individuals, the vice president of human resources, the HR representative, the training administrator, and Diane. They sat down in their little conference room and listened to the vice president, Diane's supervisor, tell them everything that she knew.

Everything she said was a repeat of what they already knew. She continued, saying, "What can we do to contribute to boosting morale instead of deflating it?" She paused and Diane thought, "Is that possible?" They discussed how individuals were still in shock, and it was going to be hard to convince them that any change was a long way off. Diane found it hard to concentrate. However, the employees were their customers, and they needed to do what was best for them. Their plan of action was to continue with business as usual: continue with their quarterly awards, continue with their weekly raffle drawings, continue filling the empty positions they had, continue with planning things for the future, and getting employees' opinions. They hoped this would show employees that they were not stopping just because things may change in the future. They also agreed to do their best to be positive when individuals asked them about the situation or what they thought. In Diane's case, she would have to lie.

The meeting ended with the department personnel discussing their fears, and what they would do if the sale went through. It was a venting session they all needed, and they knew it would be kept confidential. Diane did accomplish a little bit of work that day. But as she was walking out to her car, she thought to herself, "Who would have thought that today my future would change?" If someone had told her that her future employment would become uncertain, she would have laughed at them. She planned everything. She didn't leave important things like her employment to chance. It's amazing what one person's decision could do to so many people's lives.

Unmovable Team

by Teri C. Tompkins, University of Redlands

Paul Riley, a top executive with AVIONICS, laid his glasses on his desk and pinched the bridge of his nose. He closed his eyes and inhaled deeply. Sighing, he wondered how he was going to handle the new organization he had been handed. No, he thought, Not handed. I asked for this!

Riley had just returned from a personal meeting with the general manager of AVIONICS and he had told Riley, under no uncertain terms, that his group was under the microscope. We need new business, and we need it now! the general manager had nearly shouted. Riley could still feel the heat that crept up his face as he tried to contain his feelings of anger mixed with embarrassment. Riley had been with the new group only one year, after successfully steering another AVIONICS group into profitable waters. Riley had asked for a challenge and the general manager had given him the task of working with a slow-moving electronic sensing group. Now, Riley wasn t sure if he would be able to deliver as he had so confidently promised last year, hence the embarrassment. The anger was his frustration at the general manager for expecting such a quick turnaround in a group that had operated the same way for years.

AVIONICS

AVIONICS was a subsidiary of a large North American—based corporation named National Corporation Alliance (NCA). NCA was a market leader in a number of businesses including financial markets, real estate, and the defense industry. The defense industry units of NCA were not market leaders but were successful as a subcontractor for the leading defense industry corporations. The headquarters of the defense industry division was located in Los Angeles County in southern California.

The defense industry units of NCA had several divisions. One of the most successful had been the electronics division. The electronics division s primary focus was in the area of electronic-sensing devices, such as specialized antennas and other receivers using digital and analog technologies. AVIONICS was one of three subsidiaries in the electronics division. It was located in San Diego county in southern California. The second subsidiary, bought by NCA in the mid-1980s, was located in Silicon Valley, California. A small electronic manufacturing subsidiary, located in Colorado, was also purchased around that time.

AVIONICS was founded as a spin-off from the Los Angeles—based division when executives decided that electronic sensing was an important area that needed specialized focus. Elite engineers and top scientists were chosen to start the new venture. In the mid-1970s, property was purchased in northern San Diego County where the weather was known to be mild and the schools excellent. They built a beautiful facility, and engineers, technicians, and scientists clamored for positions.

AVIONICS did not manufacture products. Its focus was on research and development of electronic systems. The government would specify a certain type of electronic-sensing system that it needed, such as one that could hear over certain distances or distinguish voices from white noise. The engineers and scientists would then seek ways to design the product. They would build a prototype to meet the specifications and the contract would be complete. A few scientists were employed for their pure theoretical research focus. Engineers worked closely with scientists to apply the research to products.

The Nature of Defense Contracts

Although the company had grown to 1,500 employees by 1995 and had some successful contracts, it had never realized its full profit potential. AVIONICS had a good reputation, however, for designing state-of-the-art electronic sensing systems. From the mid-1970s to the late 1980s, defense contracts were such that engineers had the freedom to go above and beyond the original system specs and design better than specified systems. The government would pay for these additional costs through a system known as cost-plus (what it cost the company to make the product, plus a specified profit such as 3 percent).

Beginning in the late 1980s, the nature of contracts changed. While the companies still had to submit proposals and be competitively selected, now they had to be much more accurate about their costs because the government would no longer pay _any_ cost plus profit. The company would only be paid the amount of its bid proposal. This meant that defense contractors had to anticipate the cost of designing a new system, and had to manage costs if they expected a profit at the end of their contract. The role of project manager and other administrative functions began to take on a more significant position in AVIONICS as it struggled to contain costs and deliver on time.

Engineers, used to the creative give them more than they asked for design activities, struggled to adhere to the cost and schedule disciplines now imposed on them. Engineers felt frustrated as they were asked to coordinate more closely with each other and were told not to deliver more than promised in the contract. For some, the joy of their work was diminished as these restrictions became more and more common. In addition, many engineers complained that they did not understand what was expected of them. Trained as engineers and scientists and not as administrators, they felt confused about how to conduct business in this new environment.

Administrative overhead costs increased as administrators spent more time managing cost and schedule. Administrative overhead (AO) costs were critical to the bidding process. The lower the AO, the more successful a company would likely be in the bidding process for new contracts. AO was a function of the cost of facilities, administrators and executives, staffing, and other costs not directly related to a contract such as training, public relations, and security. AVIONICS AO was $32 per hour. Many smaller electronics firms had rates closer to $25 per hour.

When an engineer or scientist worked on a contract, he or she was required to record a job number on the weekly time card. The accounting department would track the job numbers, and that was how they kept track of each contract s costs. Whenever the employee did something that was not directly supportive of a contract, then his or her costs were charged to AO.

AVIONICS Current Business

As AVIONICS continued to struggle to reduce its AO cost, it sought additional ways to increase its profits. Top executives reasoned that if they could take some of their technological advances in electronic sensing systems to the commercial market, then they might realize greater profits. Consequently, in the early 1990s, the top executives began expecting each group within the company to find products that the public might want, and to take them commercial, if possible. The senior management team spent much of its time at its meetings discussing how this strategy should be able to help increase profits. They reasoned that if their products sold in the commercial markets, then they would be able partially to cover the costs of their highly paid engineers and scientists, and some AO costs. This would increase their ability to bid on defense contracts.

AVIONICS executives also tried one other new adventure. They opened up a small facility near their current facility, transferred a few key administrators and engineers to it, and began seeking international opportunities. The new facility was necessary for two reasons. First, security of national defense products was paramount. The new facility would not house national defense secrets. Second, the facility would have a separate budget and, therefore, AO would be significantly reduced, which would allow them to bid more competitively for international business.

The Analog Group

When Paul Riley told the general manager that he was ready for a new challenge, he was asked to work with the Analog team, a group of about 65 people responsible for leading analog (mechanisms that represent data by measurable quantities, as voltages, rather than by numbers, as with digital) engineering activities. A year ago, the group had been charged with the responsibility of not just managing the engineering activities of Analog, but also of helping the company acquire new business and increase profit.

Riley s concern was with the core group of senior engineers who managed various Analog teams. Most of the people on the management team had worked for AVIONICS since it was spun off 15 years ago. During the Cold War, these senior engineers had helped to build AVIONICS into a reasonably successful operation. Riley too had been with AVIONICS for a long time, and he considered some of the managers on this team friends. But he was feeling pressure from the general manager to find more profitable markets fast. Unfortunately, the resistance to change within the management team was high.

The management team complained to Riley that he had not defined their roles and responsibilities clearly enough. They thought the request to grow new business and add profits was too ambiguous. Riley suspected that their resistance was not related to clearly defined roles but to something else. He thought of three possibilities: (a) Fear of change or not wanting to change, (b) that at least one of the senior managers had wanted his new position, and was out there with a big stirring stick causing trouble, or (c) he had the wrong mix of people. Whatever the problem was, he was under orders to get this team in line.

Riley thought about some of the key players on his team. First, there was Dan Patrick, 54 years old. Patrick was an excellent analog electronics engineer. He was well liked by people in the Analog group. A few top managers, however, considered him an old-timer. He worked long hours, and over the years he had consistently met or exceeded all product specifications. His projects frequently ran behind schedule. While no one could argue that his group designed a good product, they could argue that he didn t manage his cost and schedule. Patrick was critical of upper management. He was known to say that top management was losing its focus on what AVIONICS had to offer to the customer, which were high quality products. He felt that too much emphasis was being placed on containing cost and schedule, no matter what the sacrifice to good products. When his former boss was transferred to the new international group, Patrick felt that due to his well-acknowledged expertise in analog systems, he was ready to take his turn at the helm of the analog group. He was disappointed in Riley s appointment because he felt that Riley didn t know enough about analog technologies.

Patrick was not the only one who thought that good products mattered, and that the company was sacrificing some of its core values in these new changes. For example, Ray Aquino was concerned because AVIONICS had a reputation for delivering good expert engineering systems to the military. Our value is our competence and our expertise. Now top management wants us to fix something that isn t broken. We re good at what we do, but top management likes to experiment. We re the guinea pigs.

Tim Ferris, senior engineer and manager, was another key player. When Riley first took over, Ferris told him, You ve got to have fun at what you are doing. Fun equals job satisfaction, which is the reason you come to work. Our team has been very effective. We work well together as a team. We ve learned to bid competitively and realistically. It took time for this to happen, but we learned it by building trust. For example: We ve convinced people that they have to be honest and tell it like it is; we ve learned that we break as a team and we succeed as a team. We ve had personality difficulties, but by and large we ve done well. No one has quit; they ve stayed in there. Everyone puts in an extraordinary amount of effort together; we ve learned to work well together. I know the skills and abilities of these guys like the back of my hand.

Tim continued, We are especially good at developing small products and applying them to system requirements that the military has. We are very competitive because we offer a good price, good capability, high performance and light weight, and good technology. That is, we can apply our skills to specific problems.

Ferris and Riley had worked together on other teams over the last 15 years. Ferris knew that Riley s preferred management style was team empowerment. That s why he was surprised at how Riley had come down hard on the management team. He had even laid off Blake Whiley, a long-time friend of both of them. Riley s management style now seemed to be directive, and often he seemed frustrated with the group.

Riley commented on his style. I really miss being one of the guys, encouraging my team, and motivating them to go further. But I can t seem to get through to these guys. Most of my management team transferred to AVIONICS from NCA s defense firm 15 years ago. They are older and will retire in the next 10 to 15 years. Except for the layoff, I don t have much to hold over their heads. They aren t motivated by money because they make a decent salary already. At AVIONICS we decide on salary and bonuses by a bonus pool divided by the top 10 percent producers. At this time, due to the depressed defense industry, the amount is only equal to 3 to 5 percent of their salary. One to 3 percent difference in their salary is not going to phase them. I have a bunch of young engineers below these guys, but they are frustrated because they don t see how they can influence decisions or manage the project. They just focus on the technical requirements, and try to stay out of the politics.

The Analog team had been reasonably successful in the past before the defense industry contracts changed. The group members were motivated by delivering good products and saving the United States of America from its enemies. Status was achieved by how good an engineer was at solving complex technical problems. Administrators were a necessary evil, and engineers could overrule an administrator by emphasizing the system requirements. Analog group members worked overtime frequently to try to stay on schedule but were more concerned with delivering the best national defense product that it could than on a small delay in scheduling. Project leaders relied on their network and credibility to manage the project s cost and schedule. If the project leader could recruit good engineering talent, and if the engineers respected the project leader, then the engineers would cooperate and work hard at satisfying their technical goals and the project leader s administrative goals.

When the nature of defense contracts changed in the late 1980s, members of the Analog team did not adjust easily, but they did eventually come around. The days of doing anything we want to do on a project is gone, says Patrick. We are learning to pay more attention to cost and schedule because that is the only way we are going to keep this company afloat.

Aquino also acknowledges how things have changed, Nowadays, if I m designing something to fit in a little black box, I check with the engineers who are designing the little black box, and make sure we are on the same page. That saves time in the end, and we are more likely to stay on schedule.

I no longer think that project leaders are superfluous, says Ferris. They have an important job to do and my job as senior management is to ensure that they have my support and clout.

It took a few years for us managers to get used to the focus of managing cost and schedule, says Riley, but I believe we have the hang of it now. Very few people would argue that cost and scheduling are not important. My challenge now is how to get these guys to look for new opportunities and new markets.

The year before Riley took over as the director of Analog, the team was told that they needed to bring in new business and increase profits, in addition to leading the engineering activity. No additional training was offered to the managers as to how to acquire new business, nor were they assigned any marketing people skilled at acquiring new business. They had received training on the financial side, including how to reduce time costs and other costs, but were not yet comfortable with looking for business outside of the defense industry.

Riley felt that he had talked, until he was blue in the face, about the need to bring in new business. This team will not focus on bringing in new business. Their continual focus is on internal research. They bid for internal jobs by underbidding, so that we lose money on the project. Once they have the project, they require resources, that is, engineers and equipment, to complete the task. Their game is to justify the use of resources to get the next project. They are very successful at this. This team seeks to maintain themselves by underbidding, thereby ensuring that the team can maintain their members and provide fun, interesting work.

Riley continues, I m not saying it s bad to enjoy your work or to be loyal to the team, but I m frustrated because the ball game has changed on these guys, and they aren t playing in the same ball park. We must bring in new business from *outside* of the firm, and we must contribute to profit. These guys are motivated by professional pride on the technical side but not the financial side, and they are motivated by self-protection. The core group members on the management team are extremely collaborative among themselves, but, I hate to say it, it reminds me of a Mafia subculture.

Riley s Dilemma

Returning from his contemplation, Riley let out another sigh and put on his glasses. It was time to go to a management meeting with the Analog management team. Riley was concerned that they had spent a large percentage of their budget, and they would run out of money before the end of the year unless they could come up with new resources. He hoped that the managers would help him think of ways to create the resources.

At the meeting, Riley explained his concern about the budget and gave his reason for the meeting. We need more money in order to pursue new business, explained Riley.

Ferris spoke up: I heard one of the managers say that the Ruby Team has done a good job controlling their costs, and that they are under budget for the year. Maybe we can steal some of theirs.

That s a great idea, said Aquino. I know of a project we can bid with them that we can piggyback on the Tactical project. That should generate enough budget to get us through.

Riley sat incredulously and looked around the room. Here is a smokestack, he thought. They sit around putting out a lot of smoke, but they are independent of all the other smokestacks. They don t think of any other group or the company as a whole, just how to protect their own. He felt he had just hit a brick wall, and he wondered how he was ever going to move this unmovable team.

Organization Chart for the Analog Group

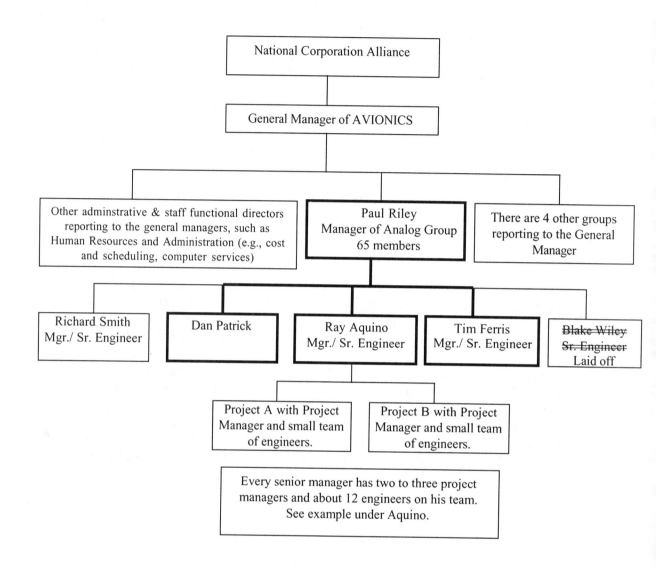

Your Uncle Wants You!

by Steven J. Maranville, University of Houston Downtown,
and J. Andrew Morris

Lt. Colonel Tyler Mason sat in his office with an expression of deep concern. For the second straight quarter, the E Recruiting Battalion of the United States Army had failed to meet its recruitment quota, although several recruiting companies within the battalion had met and exceeded expectations. Lt. Colonel Mason needed to determine the reasons for this shortfall. The report on his desk, presenting the results of a recent job satisfaction survey, offered a number of possible explanations.

The New Army

The U.S. Army was the largest of the five branches comprising the U.S. military. Consequently, the Army recruited and trained the greatest number of personnel. As a result, the recruiting function while important to all branches of the military was especially important to the Army.

In the decades since the end of the Vietnam War, the U.S. military in general, and the Army in particular, had undergone profound changes having implications for recruitment. One key change that arose from the Vietnam War experience and the antiwar movement of the 1960s was the introduction of an all volunteer force. Recruiting, which had always been important to the Army, now became essential.

Another fundamental change was the military s movement from a strategy based on sheer bulk and mass to a strategy based on flexibility and mobility. The Gulf War represented this new type of warfare fought on a regional scale and of a short-term duration. This movement toward greater flexibility and mobility required sophisticated electronic technology that, in turn, required a more educated force.

Further, since the end of the Cold War, the number of enlisted personnel in the Army had decreased through a planned downsizing. Although the total number of personnel employed by the Army was less, recruitment numbers had remained relatively stable, because turnover was high and on the increase. Fewer enlisted personnel were choosing to remain in the Army as a long-term career. Many would complete their initial tour of duty and leave with their accumulated financial savings and other benefits, such as an educational tuition reimbursement package.

Evolving societal conditions have also affected the composition of the Army s human resources. As the U.S. economy was healthy and unemployment rates were low, recruitment was more difficult. Furthermore, as the U.S. workforce became more diverse, the Army struggled to keep pace. One notable example was women in the military. To advance into leadership positions, military personnel needed to have served in combat positions; however, women, at present, were not allowed into front-line combat functions. The continued debate over the role of women in the Army made it more difficult to recruit qualified female applicants. In addition, minority groups that had historically been well represented in the Army were redefining their roles in society. Their improving level of education and broader range of career options appeared to negatively impact the extent to which minorities would consider military enlistment.

In spite of the emerging new Army, perhaps the most potent factor impacting the recruitment of enlisted personnel was a changing sense of civic duty among younger Americans. A low percentage of voter turnout and minimal participation in civic activities were indicative of a new generation that embraced different values and norms. This so-called Generation X was typified by a cynical view of life that made them pessimistic and skeptical about the need for civil service.

Volunteering for military service had traditionally appealed to those who felt an obligation to protect and defend their country. No matter how new the Army could become, its basic mission was to train people to kill other people. Hence, without a pressing need for national defense, this mission was becoming evermore difficult to sell.

The Recruiter s Job

The recruiter was tasked with making sure that there were a sufficient number of qualified personnel coming into the military to provide for the adequate defense of the nation. Military recruiters worked almost exclusively trying to fill entry-level enlisted slots, since soldiers who desired to become officers would generally self-select while in college. Training for the recruiting position involved a special 12-week program in which the would-be recruiter learned effective ways to contact prospective recruits and cultivate interest in the Army. In particular, the recruiting school focused on sales techniques that had proven effective in overcoming unfavorable attitudes regarding military service. Further, the recruiter was thoroughly instructed in all the various enlistment options and benefits programs the Army offered to enlisted personnel.

The general perception of the recruiting job in the Army was mixed. While the recruiter was often assigned to his or her hometown or other plum locations, the hours were notoriously long. In addition, serving as a recruiter had limited impact on promotion. If one wanted to advance quickly in the Army, service as a drill sergeant was considered essential, with the recruiter function a poor second. Many considered this disparity unfair, since the Army expected its recruiters to be better than the average soldier, exceeding typical Army standards regarding appearance, fitness, and service history. Essentially, recruiters put a human face on the Army by being a potential recruit s first contact. Because of its mixed reputation, only about half of recruiting positions were filled by soldiers who volunteered. The other half of the positions were filled by soldiers who had been assigned.

A recent job survey commissioned by Lt. Colonel Mason indicated that a large portion of the recruiters in his battalion were very unhappy with their positions. The comments on the survey suggested three primary reasons. First, many recruiters expressed strong resentment about having to always be on, or as one recruiter put it, putting on my happy face even when happiness is the last thing I m feeling. Second, numerous recruiters complained that the skills and abilities needed to be a good soldier did not necessarily translate into being a good spokesperson for the Army. One recruiter wrote, Dammit, I m a soldier, not a salesman; if I wanted to be a salesman, I wouldn t have joined up.

A third issue voiced by the recruiters was even more puzzling to Lt. Colonel Mason, since he was sure they were receiving excellent guidance from the chain of command. Nevertheless, a lot of the recruiters thought their 1st sergeant and company commander were out of touch with what was going on. For example, one particularly upset recruiter wrote, All anybody cares about are the numbers. The 1st Sergeant says, You gotta make the numbers for the month. But what the 1st Sergeant doesn t realize is that all that stuff about sexual harassment at the Aberdeen Proving Grounds and Fort Jackson is killing us. With all this negative press, you d have to be crazy to wanna join the Army. These feelings were echoed by another recruiter who wrote, All the 1st Sergeant wants is for us to reach quota. He doesn t care how you do it or how long it takes just bring in the numbers. But sometimes, even if you work 80 hours a week hunting down every possible lead, things don t fall into place especially now with all of this sexual-harassment craziness going on with the drill sergeants at Aberdeen. I hate this job! I can t wait to get back to the real Army!!

Mason s Decision

Lt. Colonel Mason sat brooding in his chair. In a way, he expected negative comments from some of the recruiters. Trying to make sense of the situation, he spoke aloud, Soldiers will always complain about something. It s easier to place blame somewhere else, rather than to accept responsibility for your own poor performance. The intensity and number of these comments, though, were surprising. Maybe, he continued, the anonymity of the survey just gave them a medium to blow off some steam.

Lt. Colonel Mason considered several options. First, the job satisfaction survey in itself may have solved the problem. By releasing some stress in their responses to the survey, the recruiters could now get on with their work. Second, while said in anger, some of the recruiters comments seemed legitimate and might bear looking into further. The Lt. Colonel concluded, however, The bottom line is next quarter s numbers need to be met.

<u>NOTES</u>

NOTES

<u>NOTES</u>

NOTES

NOTES

NOTES

NOTES

NOTES